D6×10 +D6	SPELL NAME	D(	
11	ASSASSIN'S DAGGER PG 58	41	GROW PG 62
12	ANIMATE PG 58	42	HURRICANE PG 62
13	AFFIX PG 58	43	HELPING HANDS PG 62
14	ASSUME SHAPE PG 58	44	ILLUSION PG 62
15	BEFUDDLE PG 59	45	INVISIBILITY PG 62
16	BREACH PG 59	46	JOLT PG 62
21	CONE OF AIR PG 60	51	LIGHT PG 63
22	BANISH SPIRIT PG 59	52	LOCK PG 63
23	EMBER PG 60	53	LANGUAGES PG 63
24	COCKROACH PG 59	54	LEVITATE PG 63
25	DARKSEE PG 60	55	SENTRY PG 66
26	DIMINISH PG 60	56	SHATTER PG 66
31	EARTHQUAKE PG 60	61	SLEEP PG 66
32	FEAR PG 61	62	THUNDER PG 67
33	FIRE BOLT PG 61	63	TONGUE TWISTER PG 67
34	FLASH PG 61	64	UNDO PG 69
35	FARSEEING PG 61	65	WARD PG 69
36	FIND PG 61	66	WALL OF POWER PG 69

Random

DAMAGE ROLL ➜	1	2	3	4	5	6	7+
Jolt	2	2	3	3	5	7	9

DAMAGE ROLL ➜	1	2	3	4	5	6	7+
Fire Bolt	3	3	5	7	9	12	16

DAMAGE ROLL ➜	1	2	3	4	5	6	7+
Dragon-Fire	6	8	12	16	18	24	36

Written by Daniel Sell.

Illustrated by Jeremy Duncan, Dirk Detweiler Leichty, Sam Mameli, and Andrew Walter.

Editing and Development by Jarrett Crader.⚜

Layout and Development by Christian Kessler.⚜

Additional Development by Daniel Martin.

Additional Editing by Brian Yaksha

Proofread by Fiona Maeve Geist⚜ and Corey Brin.⚜

Playtested by Alex Clements, Douglas Clements, Luke Gearing, Cecil Howe, Anxy P., Andrew Shipman, John Toh, Angus King, and everyone who has published a play report.

Special thanks to Christopher Mennell, Jeff Russell, Douglas Clements and Maria Rivera.

TROIKA!
Numinous Edition

CONTENTS

TABLES

Introduction

You are reading a tabletop role-playing game (RPG) in which one player takes the part of the games master (GM) and prepares the world and controls the people and peril in it while the other players create characters on a journey through that self same world.

You now have the context and key terms to explore the medium independently and nothing I say here can fully instruct you on what is a deep and rich form of entertainment on par with cinema or fly fishing. Treat it like you would any new hobby, but know that this activity is one you engage in with others. Use best practices and safety tools to ensure that everyone playing feels safe, that no unkind line is crossed, that no one is made to feel to their detriment and everyone can enjoy themselves fully.

Beyond that what you have here is TROIKA!: a science-fantasy RPG in which players travel by eldritch portal and non-euclidean labyrinth and golden-sailed barge between the uncountable crystal Spheres strung delicately across the hump-backed sky.

What you encounter on those Spheres and in those liminal places is anybody's guess — I wouldn't presume to tell you, though inside this book you will find people and artefacts from these worlds which will suggest the shape of things. The adventure and wonder are in the gaps; your game is defined by the ways in which you fill them.

Character Creation

Overview:
Go get the character sheet found on page 110.
1. Roll 1d3+3 to determine Skill.
2. Roll 2d6+12 to determine Stamina.
3. Roll 1d6+6 to determine Luck.
4. Record Baseline Possessions that every new character starts with:
   2D6 SILVER PENCE, A KNIFE, A LANTERN & FLASK OF OIL, A RUCKSACK, 6 PROVISIONS.
5. Roll d66 on the Background Table and record Possessions and Skills.

Backgrounds
Backgrounds are everything your character was before you got hold of them. They provide you with Skills, Possessions, and other Special benefits where noted. Slide into the role and make it your own.

Roll randomly to determine your starting Background. Notice that they only touch the edge of specificity: it is up to you to tailor them to the worlds you play in. Rework them or remove them entirely and replace them with your own unique vision of the Spheres. Boldly lay claim to the games you play, create content recklessly, and always write in pen.

Creating Your Own Backgrounds
When creating your own Backgrounds, as a general rule, stick to 10 or so total points distributed in a range of 1–3 with 3 being someone who has already mastered their trade. Do not dismiss the importance of a description — they are the players' window into the world — but don't feel intimidated by them. Keep them simple and pack as much information into them as you are able; when they are short and evocative the player will fill in the gaps. The Backgrounds need not be balanced or equal to one another but should instead be fun and flavourful. After making a new Background take a moment to consider the reaction of someone receiving it instead of some other entry in your particular and ever changing list. Balance the enjoyment rather than the numbers.

11 ARDENT GIANT OF CORDA
Every giant has a different story about Corda, well told and interrupted with tears and laughter, of how they lost it and mean to find it soon enough but oh, what of today? We should drink and cheer, we'll search once again in the morning!

POSSESSIONS
• An *ARTEFACT OF LOST CORDA*, being either an enormous Blue Star Map which can tell you where any portal leads (with a successful Astrology test) or a pocket barometer for forecasting the weather (5 in 6 accuracy) or a Ruby Lorgnette granting +2 Second Sight.

ADVANCED SKILLS
4 Strength
3 Astrology
2 Run
2 Climb

12 BEFOULER OF PONDS

You're a wise person, a high priest, a pond-pisser, a typical but committed adherent of P!P!Ssshrp. The bloated Toad God has no church other than the periphery of ponds where the foulness catches in the reeds, and no congregation other than the gnats and dragonflies. You minister to them all the same.

POSSESSIONS

- *SACKCLOTH ROBES,* caked in stinking mud and undergrowth. +1 to Sneak rolls in marshy terrain while wearing them, -1 everywhere else 'cos it stinks!
- *A LARGE, WORN WOODEN LADLE* (Damage as Mace).

ADVANCED SKILLS

3 Spell – Drown
3 Swim
2 Spell – Tongue Twister
2 Spell – Undo
1 Spell – Web
1 Sneak
1 Second Sight

SPECIAL

You never contract disease as a result of drinking stagnant liquids.

13 BURGLAR

As a second-story person you often have cause to wander. Enemies come naturally from both sides of the law and it pays to keep ahead of trouble.

POSSESSIONS
- CROSSBOW and *18 BOLTS*.
- Roll of LOCK PICKS.
- GRAPPLING HOOK.

ADVANCED SKILLS
2 Sneak
2 Locks
1 Awareness
1 Climb
1 Trapping
1 Knife Fighting
1 Crossbow Fighting

SPECIAL

You may Test your Luck to find and get in with the local criminal underbelly if one exists.

14 CACOGEN

You are Those-Filthy-Born, spawned in the hump-backed sky lit only by great black anti-suns and false light. Your mother was sailing on the golden barges or caught in some more abstract fate when she passed you, far from the protective malaise of the million Spheres. You were receptive to the power and the glory at a generative time and it shows in your teratoid form.

POSSESSIONS
- *FUSIL.*
- *2D6 PLASMIC CORES.*
- *SWORD.*
- *VELARE.*

ADVANCED SKILLS
2 Fusil Fighting
2 Astrology
2 Second Sight
2 Spell – Random
2 Spell – Random
2 Golden Barge Pilot
1 Spell – Random
1 Sword Fighting

15 Chaos Champion

You no longer don the spiked brass armour but you still have the ear of your Chaos patron. They're happy for you to experiment with not plunging your world into disorder and, ultimately, darkness, but the door is always open.

Possessions
- *Ritual Scars.*
- *A Huge Maul.*
- Assortment of *Ragged Armour* (counts as Modest Armour).
- *Dream Journal*, almost full.

Advanced Skills
6 Language – Kurgan
3 Maul Fighting
3 Secret Signs – Chaos Patron
1 Spell – Random
1 Second Sight

Special
Name your patron. You may call upon your patron for aid once per day. To do so roll three 6s on 3d6. The GM interprets their intervention.

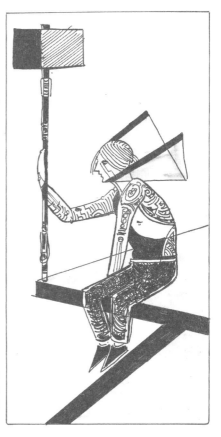

16 CLAVIGER

The Key Masters wander the universe fathoming the workings of all entryways. Though they're quite fascinated with simple chests and doors they are most excited by metaphysical and metaphorical barriers. You might find small conclaves of Clavigers camped around the feet of Demon Gates, debating appropriate methods of attack and building obscure machines of entry.

POSSESSIONS
- Festooned with *KEYS* (counts as Modest Armour).
- A *DISTINGUISHED SLEDGEHAMMER* (Damage as Maul).
- *LOCK PICKING TOOLS.*

ADVANCED SKILLS
4 Locks
3 Strength
3 Trapping
2 Spell – Open
1 Spell – See Through
1 Maul Fighting
1 Spell – Lock

21 DEMON STALKER

You stake your reputation upon your ability to hunt and kill demonic creatures and those who break bread with them. Be it Goatmen in the wilds or the Angel cults of the slums, all need to be driven back off the edge of the map and onto the shores of chaos.

POSSESSIONS
- *A SILVER SWORD.*
- *16 SILVER ARROWS* and *BOW.*
- *POUCH OF SALT.*
- *VIAL OF DEMON BLOOD.*

ADVANCED SKILLS
5 Language – Abyssal
3 Spell – Blood Shroud
2 Second Sight
2 Sword Fighting
2 Bow Fighting
1 Tracking
1 Sneak

22 Dwarf

You are a short, hairy, belligerent creature. Dwarfs are a fabricated people, each made in turn by another, and as such there are no Dwarf children or Dwarf parents to prevent you from fully committing to the important Dwarfy endeavours of creating fine art in unusual places. You intend to find the most unusual places in all the Million Spheres.

POSSESSIONS
- *MASONRY HAMMER.*
- *ROLL OF ARTIST'S SUPPLIES.*

ADVANCED SKILLS
3 Awareness
2 Sculpting
2 Painting
2 Metalworking
2 Construction
2 Strength
2 Fist Fighting
2 Wrestling
1 Hammer Fighting

SPECIAL
Dwarfs may eat gems and rare metals as food replacements. You, in fact, vastly prefer the taste of rare minerals to mundane food.

23 Epopt

You are a roaming seer, selling your foresight at local fetes where you are instantly recognisable by your yellow coif and habit as being open for business. Road weary and worldwise, your unpopular visions cause you to constantly move on.

Possessions

- *Yellow epopt outfit*, padded for protection against unhappy clients (counts as Modest Armour).
- *Epopt Staff*, being a walking staff with seeing crystal on one end (Damage as Staff).
- *Collapsible tent*, large enough for your stall.

Advanced Skills

2 Awareness
2 Evaluate
1 Second Sight
1 Etiquette
1 Fist Fighting
1 Run

Special

Epopts may Test their Luck to get a yes or no answer to a question about mundane matters. The GM should make this Test in private, not informing the Epopt if their visions are accurate.

24 Exographer

Where you come from it's become quite normal to traverse the Spheres. Idle academics like yourself have even begun to study these more remote reaches of the divine effluvia. Though these rural indwellers may never appreciate your important work, you thanklessly measure their latent phlogiston for posterity.

Possessions
- *Hermetically Sealed Rubber Suit* (counts as Heavy Armour)
- *Exographical Surveyors Box*
- *Spring-Loaded Measuring Tape*
- *Pistolet*
- *1d6 Plasmic Cores*

Advanced Skills
4 Exography
3 Golden Barge Pilot
2 Astrology
2 Pistolet Fighting

25 THE FELLOWSHIP OF KNIDOS
Mathmologists honour the clean and unambiguous truths of mathematics and coordinate them with their observations of the Spheres. All things can be measured and predicted with the application of the correct mathmological ratios, those methods applied to penetrate the ethereal surface and glimpse the fundamental numbers below.

POSSESSIONS
- *LARGE ASTROLABE* (Damage as Mace).
- *ABACUS.*
- *LOTS OF SCROLLS* and *WRITING EQUIPMENT.*

ADVANCED SKILLS
3 Mathmology
2 Astrology
2 Spell – Find

26 FELLOW OF THE PEERAGE OF PORTERS & BASIN FILLERS

Luggers are a servile group by nature, most often found in the service of others, weighed down by loads that would buckle a donkey. You take pride in this, so much so that the everyday assignments of the guild cannot sate your desire to serve, causing you to venture out in search of a real challenge for such a talented varlet.

POSSESSIONS
- *A WOODEN YOKE.*
- *BROWN OVERCOAT* and *SOFT DOFFING CAP OF THE GUILD.*
- *A BALE HOOK* (Damage as Knife and +1 on rolls to lift heavy objects).
- *LENGTH OF ROPE.*

ADVANCED SKILLS
4 Strength
2 Fist Fighting
2 Run
1 Hook Fighting
1 Sneak
1 Awareness

31 GREMLIN CATCHER

No matter what country, Sphere, or abstract dimension you may find yourself in, be assured that gremlins are there, digging their warrens and bothering nice people willing to pay you a shiny penny to bash their little heads in.

POSSESSIONS
- *SMALL BUT VICIOUS DOG.*
- *FLAT CAP.*
- *A CLUB.*
- *A SACK.*
- *1D6 EMPTY GREMLIN JARS.*
- *A JAR WITH A PISSED-OFF GREMLIN INSIDE.*

ADVANCED SKILLS
4 Tunnel Fighting
4 Trapping
2 Sneak
2 Awareness
2 Club Fighting
2 Tracking
1 Swim

32 JOURNEYMAN OF THE GUILD OF SHARP CORNERS

You are an assassin in training, graduated from fighting dummies and branding practise clients, freshly imbued with a license to ply your trade. You haven't fully developed the idiosyncratic methods required of a master but you are on the path.

POSSESSIONS
- *BLACK CLOTHES OF THE APPRENTICE.*
- *GARROTTE.*
- *CURVED SWORD.*
- *3 VIALS OF POISON.*
- *CROSSBOW* and *6 BOLTS.*

ADVANCED SKILLS
1 Poison
1 Sneak
1 Locks
1 Knife Fighting
1 Climb
1 Awareness
1 Crossbow Fighting
1 Swim
1 Disguise

33 LANSQUENET

You are a mercenary retained in the exclusive service of the Phoenix Throne, handsomely paid and sent to distant Spheres on golden ships to spread the ineffable glory of your lords at the tip of your flaming sword.

POSSESSIONS
- *EXQUISITE PISTOLET.*
- *BANDOLIER* containing *18 PLASMIC CORES.*
- *GREATSWORD.*
- *BRIGHTLY COLOURED CLOTHING* with lots of tassels and bells (impossible to sneak). Though frivolous looking it is in fact built with the Autarch's divine alchemy and considered Modest Armour while weighing the same as normal clothing (takes no slots in your inventory).

ADVANCED SKILLS
2 Greatsword Fighting
2 Pistolet Fighting
1 Run
1 Fist Fighting
1 Astrology

34 LONESOME MONARCH

You were the ruler of all you surveyed, a great conqueror, a lawbringer! Unfortunately your horse sped off into the pixie forest, or the court magician ensured you disappeared, or you led a sortie into the stars to put your stamp on them as well. Either way you are now a lost and lonely sovereign without a kingdom — no one has heard of you or your people. Most don't believe you and laugh, or worse, they do believe you and shrug at the vagaries of fate.

POSSESSIONS
- *NICE WEAPON* of your choice.
- *CROWN.*
- *TIRED HORSE.*

ADVANCED SKILLS
3 Etiquette
3 Fighting in your Nice Weapon
3 Ride
1 Tracking

35 MEMBER OF MISS KINSEY'S DINING CLUB
The Eaters know that there are only two worlds: the Without and the Within. They intend to insert as much of the prior into the latter as they can while experiencing the finest delights available. All culinary experience is open to them as nothing is forbidden at Miss Kinsey's. Try the other, other, other white meat.

POSSESSIONS
- *SHARP METAL DENTURES* (Damage as Sword) or *FORKED METAL DENTURES* (Damage as Knife. On a Mighty Blow you may cleanly strip all the flesh from one small appendage) or *BLUNT METAL DENTURES* (Damage as Knife. May be used to eat hard objects).
- *EMBROIDERED NAPKIN.*

ADVANCED SKILLS
3 Etiquette
1 Strength
1 Tracking
1 Trapping
1 Gastrology

SPECIAL
Eaters are immune to mundane ingested poisons. They may also identify any object if eaten, gaining knowledge of its material, its origin (if plausibly familiar), and its magical properties on a successful Test of Gastrology though the object must be thoroughly masticated, not merely swallowed and passed. This does not grant special immunity to any effects the object may possess.

36 MONKEYMONGER

Life on The Wall is hard. One is never more than a few yards from an endless fall yet those precarious villages still need to eat. This is where you come in with your Edible Monkeys (the distinction is purely for appeal since all monkeys are of course edible). You used to spend days on end dangling your feet off the edge of the world, watching over your chittering livestock while they scampered hither and thither, but there was no future in monkey meat. You wanted much more and so stepped off. Or you fell off. Either way you and some unlucky monkeys are here now and that's all that matters.

POSSESSIONS
- *MONKEY CLUB.*
- *BUTCHER'S KNIFE.*
- *1D6 SMALL MONKEYS* that do not heed commands but are too scared and hungry to travel far from you.
- *A POCKET FULL OF MONKEY TREATS.*

ADVANCED SKILLS
4 Climb
2 Trapping
1 Club Fighting
1 Knife Fighting

SPECIAL
The GM may choose to roll on this table anytime the Mien of monkeys must be determined.

MIEN	
1	Playful
2	Stalking
3	Hungry
4	Tired
5	Austere
6	Aggressive

41 NECROMANCER

The least popular of magical practitioners, Necromancers are shunned by the major centres of learning, left to their own devices on the edges of society, passing on knowledge in the time honoured master–student dynamic. This loneliness encourages students to make their own friends.

POSSESSIONS

- *DUSTY ROBES.*
- *THE SKULL OF YOUR MASTER* or
- *ZOMBIE SERVANT* or *GHOST* with whom you have developed a codependent relationship.

ADVANCED SKILLS

2 Healing
2 Mortuary Science
2 Relationship Counseling
1 Spell – Posthumous Vitality
1 Spell – Skeletal Counsel
1 Spell – Torpor
1 Sneak

42 PARCHMENT WITCH

Known for their smooth skin, midnight gatherings, and preternatural fear of rain and open flames; the Parchment Witches are long-dead sorcerers who cannot give up the vanity of life. They cover themselves in perfect paper skin, a patiently painted and immaculately folded imitation of life intended to hide ancient bone and gristle.

POSSESSIONS
- *D6 ROLLS OF PARCHMENT.*
- *VIALS OF PIGMENTS* and *POWDERS.*
- *COLLECTION OF BRUSHES.*
- *SWORD CANE.*

ADVANCED SKILLS
2 Spell – Protection From Rain
2 Spell – Callous Strike
2 Spell – Quench
2 Spell – True Seeing
2 Disguise
2 Second Sight
1 Healing
1 Spell – Undo
1 Spell – Random

SPECIAL

You are undead and so do not need to breathe or circulate blood. You take double Damage from Silver Weapons and regain Stamina half as effectively from all sources. You must Test your Luck if outside in the rain, are made wet, are close to open flames, or suffer generally grievous wounds. A failure sees your skin ruined. If your skin is compromised you are very obviously a walking corpse.

43 DERIVATIVE DWARF

Dwarfs are known for being the finest artisans of the Million Spheres. Give a Dwarf a rock and they will make gold, give a Dwarf a boulder and they will make a Dwarf. You were supposed to be the finest expression of Dwarfy craftsmanship, a true masterpiece, a brand new Dwarf like no other, but you were deemed a failure and left unfinished.

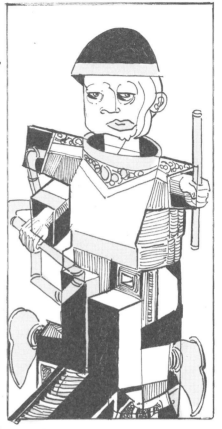

POSSESSIONS
- WOODSMAN'S AXE.
- EMPTY FIRKIN.

ADVANCED SKILLS
3 Fist Fighting
3 Awareness
2 Strength
2 Wrestling
2 Axe Fighting

SPECIAL
As 22 Dwarf but additionally:

To non-Dwarfy eyes you look like any other Dwarf, only Dwarfs can see the flaws in your creation. Other Dwarfs will completely ignore you, not out of spite but out of utter disinterest. You have +4 Sneak versus Dwarfs.

44 QUESTING KNIGHT

You are on a quest for the grail, or the sword, or the throne, or for God, or a lost love, or some other regionally significant aspirational device. Your sort are common enough, wandering the Spheres, acting out your romantic melodrama and accusing good folk of being demons or faeries. Generally considered to be harmless.

POSSESSIONS
- *HEAVY ARMOUR.*
- *HORSE.*
- *LANCE* (Damage as Spear).
- *SWORD.*
- *SHIELD.*
- *A QUIXOTIC UNDERTAKING.*

ADVANCED SKILLS
3 Jousting
2 Sword Fighting
2 Spear Fighting
1 Shield Fighting
1 Awareness

45 RED PRIEST

You are a katabolic evangelist of the Red Redemption, wandering confessor, a cauterizer of the festering wound of sin — the accumulation of Mass. Only by rejecting all earthly matter can one be unshackled to the density which binds them to the demiurge

POSSESSIONS
- *RED ROBES.*
- *TRADITIONAL FACELESS METAL HELMET* of your order (Modest Armour).
- *SYMBOLIC (BUT FULLY SIZED AND FULLY FUNCTIONAL) SINGLE HEADED GREATAXE*, to help batter down the door to sin (Damage as Greatsword).

ADVANCED SKILLS
2 Spell – Ember
2 Spell – Fire Bolt
2 Spell – Flash
2 Great Axe Fighting
1 Second Sight
1 Spell – Exorcism

46 RHINO-MAN

The original Rhino-Men were created by a lonely sorcerer several centuries ago. Even though the sorcerer has long since died of old age their profound sense of loyalty and total lack of imagination ensures most of them still guard him to this day.

POSSESSIONS
• *HORN* (Damage as Knife).
• *THICK SKIN* (Rhino Men always count as being Modestly Armoured).
• *UNDERSIZED SPEAR.*
• *TINY, USELESS HELMET.*
• *KNUCKLE DICE.*
• *HALF FULL FIRKIN OF RHINO-BEER*
• (20 Provisions worth).

ADVANCED SKILLS
3 Spear Fighting
2 Run
2 Strength
1 Gambling

51 SCEPTICAL LAMASSU

With the body of a bull, the head of a man, the forelegs of a cat, and the wings of a swan you are the sweetest of the children of the gods. You, however, were not content to rest on your cloud and instead descended from the heavens or crawled up from the abyss and set about finding your own path among the stars.

POSSESSIONS

- *INCIDENTAL SACRED JEWELLERY* worth 10d6 Silver pence if traded.
- *PILLBOX HAT.*
- *CLAWS* (Damage as Sword).
- *HOOVES* (Damage as Club).
- *WINGS* — able to fly as fast as a running man over clear ground.

ADVANCED SKILLS

3 Fly
3 Spell – Random
3 Spell – Random
3 Spell – Random
2 Claw Fighting
1 Hoof Fighting

52 Sorcerer of the Academy of Doors
You are a student at Troika's most prestigious wizarding academy (pride of the city, experts in pan-dimensional mobility) you were finally able to penetrate the (2d6)th door. You are no master but few outside your peers can claim to know more about the vagaries of skyward travel than you.

Possessions
- *Small Functional Door* worn on your forehead through which you channel your magic.
- *Flashy Robes.*

Advanced Skills
3 Astrology
2 Second Sight
2 Spell – Astral Reach
1 Spell – Teleport
1 Spell – Web
1 Spell – Random
1 Spell – Random
1 Spell – Random

53 SORCERER OF THE COLLEGE OF FRIENDS
As an integral part of your tutelage in the sub-dimensional academy of the Cordial Wizard God you spent your childhood learning about the fate of pixies, the colour of magic, ritual grammar, and endless other theoretical topics. Now you're out in the world, discovering that your education hardly accounted for any of the things that you've seen.

POSSESSIONS
- *POINTED WIZARD HAT* you received at graduation.
- *POCKET FULL OF WIZARD BISCUITS* (2d6, each counts as a Provision).
- *WAND* used to help focus new apprentices, now kept for sentimental reasons.

ADVANCED SKILLS
4 Secret Signs – Witching Words
2 Run
1 Climb
1 Sleight of Hand
1 Swim
1 Sneak
1 Second Sight
1 Spell – Jolt
1 Spell – Amity
1 Spell – Mirror Selves
1 Spell – Protection from Rain
1 Spell – Helping Hands
1 Spell – Purple Lens
1 Spell – Random

54 Fellow of The Sublime Society of Beef Steaks

Brawlers believe the application of might and a good beef steak is the universal truth. Words have no power and can no more define the universe than they can build a house, lift a cup, or sear a steak. Might can! Really, they have thought a lot about this.

Possessions
- *Weapon* of your choice.
- *Small Gridiron.*
- *2kg of Premium Meat Cuts.*
- *Waistcoat.*
- *Bottle of Strong but Fancy Wine.*

Advanced Skills
2 in a Fighting Skill of your choice
2 Wrestling
2 Swim
2 Climb
2 Run
2 Fist Fighting
1 Grilling

55 TEMPLE KNIGHT OF TELAK

THE SWORDBRINGER

You were once (and possibly still are) a fanatical monk set to maintain constant, vigilant martial readiness in preparation for the end times, when all doorways crumble inwards. You are always prepared and never unready.

POSSESSIONS

- *THE BLESSING OF TELAK.*
- *6 SWORDS* of your choice.

ADVANCED SKILLS

3 Awareness
2 Blacksmithing
1 Sword Fighting
1 Greatsword Fighting

SPECIAL

The blessing of Telak awards you Armour equal to half (rounded down) the number of Swords you carry. If you carried 6 Swords your Armour would be 3 while if you carried 9 it would be 4.

You must be overtly armed at all times or Telak takes this blessing away until you forge and donate to the unarmed a brand new Sword.

56 THAUMATURGE

Wandering miracle workers, the depths of whose clothes are filled with pouches of unguents, holy icons and herbs. No matter the metaphysical need, you are always prepared.

POSSESSIONS
- *THAUMATURGIC FEZ.*
- *STAFF*, bedecked with charms and bells. May reroll one die on the Oops! Table if using this staff, however, may never sneak up on anyone because of the ringing and clattering it makes.
- *CURLED SHOES.*
- *VOLUMINOUS ROBES.*

ADVANCED SKILLS
3 Spell – Undo
2 Spell – Assume Shape
2 Spell – Thunder
2 Spell – Random
1 Spell – Brittle Twigs
1 Spell – Random
1 Second Sight
1 Astrology

SPECIAL
You may Test your Luck to just so happen to have exactly the (common) mystic tchotchke, bauble, or gewgaw the situation requires.

61 THINKING ENGINE

Your eyes are dull ruby Spheres, your skin is hard and smooth like ivory but brown and whorled like wood. You are clearly broken, you have no memory of your creation or purpose, and some days your white internal juices ooze thickly from cracks in your skin.

POSSESSIONS
- *SOLDERING IRON.*
- *DETACHABLE AUTONOMOUS HANDS* or *CENTAUR BODY* (+4 Run) or *INBUILT PARTICLE DETECTOR* (+4 Second Sight) or *ONE RANDOM SPELL AT RANK 3.*

ADVANCED SKILLS
3 Golden Barge Pilot
2 Astrology
2 Pistolet Fighting
2 Healing
1 Run
1 Strength
1 Cooking

SPECIAL
You don't recover Stamina by resting in the usual manner — instead you must spend a full rest period with a hot iron welding your skin back together like putty. For each hour of rest with access to the right tools you regain 3 Stamina.

You may recharge plasmic machines by hooking your fluids to them and spending Stamina at a rate of 1 Stamina and 6 minutes per charge.

You always count as being at least Lightly Armoured.

62 VENGEFUL CHILD

Your village was burnt down by ruffians, or your mother was beheaded by snake cultists, or your father was hung by corrupt officials. Either way you took umbrage and entered the world with a chip on one shoulder and an oversized Sword on the other.

POSSESSIONS

- *TOO-LARGE SWORD* that provides +1 to Longsword Fighting and Damage while using it. Only you may benefit from this bonus; it's not magic, just sentimental.
- *OLD HUNTING BOW* and *12 ARROWS*.

ADVANCED SKILLS

3 Longsword Fighting
1 Awareness
1 Climb
1 Bow Fighting
1 Run
1 Swim
1 Vengeance

63 VENTURESOME ACADEMIC

You're a classically trained Academic, a product of the universities of the Brass City, the Palace of Tigers, or some other less prestigious centre of learning among the Spheres.

POSSESSIONS

- *READING GLASSES* in a sturdy case (you cannot read without them).
- *SMALL SWORD.*
- *BUNDLE OF CANDLES AND MATCHES.*
- *WRITING MATERIALS.*
- *JOURNAL.*

ADVANCED SKILLS

2 Evaluate
2 Astrology
1 Healing
1 Spell – Random
1 Sword Fighting
1 Sleight of Hand

SPECIAL

You may Test your Luck to recall facts that you might reasonably be expected to have encountered relating to the natural sciences and humanities.

64 WIZARD HUNTER

Some people say man is the most dangerous prey. They're wrong. Can men ignite the air and freeze your blood? Can men turn into flocks of seagulls when cornered in an alley? No, they can't. Wizards are the most dangerous prey.

POSSESSIONS
- *LARGE SACK.*
- *WITCH-HAIR ROPE.*
- *CROSSBOW* and *12 BOLTS.*
- *SWORD.*
- *1D6 POCKET GODS.*
- *RUBY LORGNETTE.*

ADVANCED SKILLS
2 Tracking
2 Disguise
2 Crossbow Fighting
1 Sword Fighting
1 Sneak
1 Locks
1 Etiquette

65 Yongardy Lawyer

Down in Yongardy they do things differently. They respect the Law. Every day there is a queue outside the courts to get a seat to see the latest up and coming barrister defend their case with a metre of steel. The people follow the careers of their favourite solicitors, watch all their cases, collect their portraits, and sneak into the court after hours to dab the patches of blood on white handkerchiefs.

In Yongardy, they love the Law.

Possessions

- *Rapier* (Damage as Sword) and *Puffy Shirt* or *Sjambok* (Damage as Club) and *Lots of Scars* or *Longsword* and *Heavy Armour* or *Hammer* and *Gargantuan Shield*.
- *Manual on Yongardy Law*.
- *Barrister's Wig*.

Advanced Skills

4 Fighting in your chosen Weapon
2 Etiquette
1 Healing

66 ZOANTHROP

At some point in your past you decided you didn't need it anymore: you found a Zoanthropologist and paid them well to remove your troublesome forebrain and elevate you to the pure and unburdened beast you are today.

POSSESSIONS

• No starting possessions; you have thrown off the shackles of civilisation. You are probably nude.

ADVANCED SKILLS

3 Climb
3 Run
2 Strength
2 Fist Fighting
2 Club Fighting
2 Wrestling

SPECIAL

You are immune to all mind altering effects. You are able to speak but usually choose not to. When making Advancement Checks for Skills related to abstract thought, such as Spells or Astrology, you must roll twice and succeed on both to improve them.

The Rules

1. Rolling the Dice

There is only one die type used in Troika!, that being the d6. This can be used as a d3, d6, d66, d666, and so on. To roll a d3 just roll a d6 and halve it, rounding up. To roll a d66, d666, or more just roll a d6 as many times, in order, as there are 6s. So a d66 would be a d6 followed by another d6 (e.g. I roll a 1 then roll a 4 thus making a roll of 14).

To do most actions you'll be required to roll 2d6, adding them together, as a Roll Under or a Roll Versus.

1.1 Roll Under

Rolling Under is the throwing of 2d6 with the intention of scoring equal to or under a number. This is mainly used in unopposed situations like climbing a wall or casting a Spell. Rolling two 6s always results in failure.

1.2 Roll Versus

Roll Versus, mostly used for combat or other contests, occurs when two opponents each roll 2d6, add any applicable bonuses, then compare results, the higher total winning. In a duel you might be rolling 2d6 plus your Sword Fighting total, looking to beat your opponent who is doing similar.

2. Advanced Skills & Spells

Characters have a variety of Advanced Skills & Spells granted them by their Background. The number given in the Background plus their Skill is referred to as their Skill Total. Write this on the character sheet.

2.1 Testing Advanced Skills & Spells

Most Tests of Advanced Skills & Spells are Roll Under (12 & 14).

> 2.1.1 When you successfully Test an Advanced Skill or Spell, put a tick next to it on your character sheet. These are used to Get Better (11.1).

3. Luck

Of all the numbers on your character sheet, Luck is likely to fluctuate the most. This number represents your character's fortune and intuition, tested whenever fate swipes at them. When this happens the GM will ask you to Test your Luck or suffer the consequences.

3.1 Testing your Luck

Roll equal to or less than your current Luck score. Every time you Test your Luck, reduce your current Luck score by 1 regardless of whether the Test was successful or not. Testing your Luck is optional; you may always refuse to roll and instead accept your fate. The GM is not obliged to give you details of the consequences if they are not already obvious.

3.2 Gaining and Losing Luck

For every 8 hours rest you may regain 2d6 Luck. Luck may not exceed the starting value rolled at character creation save for exceptional situations. Running out of Luck inflicts no special penalty.

3.3 Use of Luck in Combat

In the case of a tie the character may Test their Luck to break it in their favour. When a character successfully hits an opponent, but before rolling for Damage, they may decide to Test their Luck and, if successful, may add 2 to their Damage Roll.

3.4 OPTIONAL: Luck Versus Death

If you find your games are too fatal and that the turnover of characters is too much to bear the GM might optionally allow characters who have died to Test their Luck and, instead of dying, be incapacitated, wounded, or saved by some bizarre twist of fate.

4. Stamina

4.1 Running Out of Stamina

When reduced to 0 Stamina you are in danger of dying and must be healed in order to survive. If this is during an Initiative Round the next time the End of the Round Token is drawn you die. If this happens out of Initiative your friends have one opportunity to Heal you (restoring you to 1 Stamina) or else YOU ARE DEAD.

4.2 Healing

You regain 2d6 Stamina if you sleep for 8 hours. You may also eat a Provision to regain 1d6 Stamina. A maximum of 3 Provisions per day provide healing benefits. There may be other forms of healing available at your GM's discretion such as visiting bath houses or drinking potions. You may never have more Stamina than your starting total.

4.3 Negative Stamina

If you ever go below 0 Stamina you are dead.

4.4 Death

You may immediately make a new character while others mourn your loss and fight over your possessions. This new character starts exactly according to the rules found at the beginning of this book.

5. Initiative

5.1 Assemble the Stack

During combat, or at other times where it is important to know who goes first, you need to assemble the Initiative Stack. To do this get a container and a selection of coloured dice or other convenient markers (consider cards, poker chips, and so on).

5.1.1 Assign each character 2 Tokens of a single color.

5.1.2 Add Tokens to the Stack for the enemies equal to their total combined Initiative (if you have 8 Lizard-Men (Initiative 2) you would add 16 tokens to the Stack).

5.1.3 Add 1 Token of a distinct colour to the Stack. This Token signifies the End of the Round.

5.1.4 OPTIONAL: Enemy Initiative Limit. It is very likely that sometimes the characters' enemies grossly outnumber them, and make it very hard for them to act. The GM may optionally limit the number of Enemy Initiative Tokens placed in the Stack to double that which the characters contribute. So if a party of 5 (10 Initiative Tokens in total) is attacked by fifty goblins (50 Initiative Tokens) the goblins only contribute 20 Tokens to the Stack. Bear in mind that the GM should feel free to balance Initiative Stacks as it seems appropriate.

5.2 Using the Stack

The GM removes a Token from the Stack at random, the colour or design of which determines who holds the Initiative and takes a Turn. Consider giving a copy of their Token to each player so that everyone remembers which colour or design is theirs.

5.3 End of the Round

If the End of the Round Token is drawn all Tokens, including the End of the Round Token, are put back in the Stack. Remove Tokens contributed by dead characters and enemies, resolve any per Round or end of Round activities such as magic effects, Drowning (7.9), fire, poison, or bleeding, then draw another Token and carry on.

5.4 Henchmen

Hired help that are willing to engage in combat each provide 1 Initiative Token to the Stack. Henchmen share a single colour Token and when a henchman Token is drawn the GM determines who acts and what they do. The GM should take the wishes of the players under advisement but act in the best interests of the henchman.

5.5 Enemies

All enemies contribute a varying number of Initiative Tokens to the Initiative Stack according to their combined Initiative and share the same colour or design. When drawing an enemy Initiative Token the GM can declare that any enemy is acting, including an enemy who has acted previously this Round. Obviously this can be abused for mechanical gain on the GM's part though that would be entirely to the detriment of the game and is discouraged. Apply Initiative Tokens as they make sense.

5.6 Rationale

The random Turn length adds a degree of uncertainty where you never know how much time you have left. When actions are not taking place it represents hesitation, panic, or other incidental delays that can happen in a tense encounter where every second counts. The goblins have few Tokens because they are cowardly, not because they are slow; the dragon has many because it knows exactly what it wants, not because it is fast.

6. Actions

When you hold the Initiative you may take a Turn and can generally perform one action. The following list is not exhaustive and the GM is encouraged to interpret player intentions as best they can.

6.1 Hit Someone

To stab, bludgeon, or otherwise physically interfere with someone, Roll (2d6+Skill+Advanced Skill) Versus an opponent doing the same thing. The winner Rolls for Damage and the loser deducts the number generated by the Damage Roll from their Stamina. Note that either party in any exchange can potentially win. In a tie both parties have avoided hurting each other. Also note that this means you can potentially hit an unlimited number of people in a Round but may only Initiate once per Turn.

6.2 Shoot Someone

Shooting an opponent is resolved by Rolling Versus their Skill or appropriate evasive Advanced Skill such as Shield or Dodge.

6.2.1 Shooting Into Melee.
When shooting into melee on a successful hit assign a number to every individual involved and roll a die. If their number comes up they receive the Damage.

6.2.2 Aim.
On your Turn you may decide to take Aim with your ranged Weapon. To do so hold onto your Initiative Token. When your next Initiative Token is drawn you may roll twice and pick the best roll. If the End of the Round Token comes up and you haven't used your Aim Token you may decide to hold onto it for the next Round.

6.3 Cast a Spell

Each Spell has its own instructions on how it should be used but in general you need to spend a certain amount of Stamina and Roll Under or Roll Versus (for Spells that require you to touch an unwilling party, for instance) in order to create some kind of effect. Unless the Spell says otherwise it requires at least one hand free and the ability to speak. Roll on the Oops! Table if the result is a Fumble.

6.4 Delay

You may choose not to act when you hold Initiative. In that case put your Token back in the Stack.

6.5 Move

Every action is assumed to have a bit of movement involved. Anything less than 4 metres is folded into whatever else you might be doing. If you wish to chase after someone or perform some other involved locomotion then just spend a Turn doing it.

6.6 Retrieve an Item

If you need to get something out that you weren't already holding in your hands roll 2d6 and score equal to or higher than its position on your Inventory list. If you succeed you can pull it out and do what you intended. Otherwise you spend your entire action finding it. Double 1s always indicate a failure.

Retrieving an arrow counts as an item retrieval. Make sure they're packed on top! See Sections 10.3 and 10.4.1 for more on Inventories.

6.7 Use an Item

If an item is in your hands you may use it however you like (6.6).

6.8 Grapple

Roll Versus your opponent's Wrestling Skill. If you win you may either knock them to the ground or deal Damage as Unarmed and knock you both to the ground (from throwing or tackling them). On a Mighty Blow (7.4) you render them unconscious for 1d6 Rounds. If you fail to grapple them they may deal Damage to you as though they had attacked you normally whereas if you Fumble (7.5) they deal you a Mighty Blow.

7. Other Concerns

7.1 Cover
When attacking someone in cover they receive a bonus to their roll to not be hit. Consider a waist high bush to be +1 while a castle's crenulations would be +6.

7.2 Enemies
Mechanically speaking, an opponent is typically reduced to three numbers: Skill, Stamina, and Initiative. Beyond this they may have an Advanced Skill or two or some peculiar special rules.

7.3 Hitting Someone Unawares
If your opponent is not aware of your presence your attack is a Roll Under rather than a Roll Versus (1.2), they may not attack back, and you may add 2 to your Damage Roll.

7.4 Mighty Blows
If you roll a double 6 while attacking you strike a Mighty Blow, win the exchange, and inflict Double Damage (8.1). If both parties strike a Mighty Blow a spectacular clinch is formed, shattering both Weapons (in the case of beastly claws, tentacles, and so on they lose 1d6 Stamina instead).

7.5 Fumbles
A roll of double 1s in combat results in the roller losing the exchange and their opponent adding 1 to their Damage Roll. If both parties Fumble they each deal Damage to the other, adding 1 to their Damage Roll.

7.6 Shields
Shields reduce Damage Rolls by 1 to a minimum of 1.

7.7 Use of Multiple Weapons
When rolling Damage you may choose which Weapon to reference the Damage Roll against after rolling. You must be holding it in your hands or nearest approximations, obviously.

7.8 Falling Over
When on the floor you suffer -2 to all physical rolls against those standing, including Damage Rolls, and must spend a Turn getting to your feet.

7.8.1 Falling Too Far. When engaging in uncontrolled falls you lose 1d6 Stamina per 2 metres fallen when you land.

7.9 Drowning

When you fail a Swimming Test you begin to Drown and lose 1d6 Stamina. For each consecutive Swimming Test where you make no progress you roll an additional 1d6. So for instance your third failed Swimming roll in a row would lose you 3d6 Stamina. Once you lose all Stamina you have Drowned.

7.9.1 Fire, Poison, and Bleeding. Any ongoing debilitating effects should be treated similarly to Drowning. Unless you have a specific effect in mind have the victim lose 1d6 Stamina per Turn with it optionally becoming more severe unless they either pass a related Advanced Skill Test or successfully Test their Luck (or Skill for Enemies). Improvisation is strongly encouraged.

7.9.2 Degenerative Effects in Combat. Test for Drowning, fire, etc. only when the End of the Round Token is drawn.

7.10 Henchmen

Henchmen are created as you would a monster, with truncated abilities only covering their essence. They are their own people with their own motivations and are not just pieces of equipment. It is up to the GM and players to flesh them out or not as the case may be. Also see Section 5.4.

7.11 Time

There are two main units of time in the game: Turns and Rounds. A Turn is what someone does when they hold Initiative and is a few seconds long. A Round is the period between drawing successive End of the Round Tokens and is roughly equal to one minute.

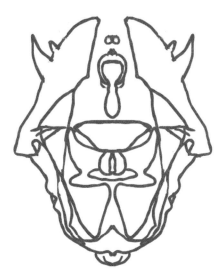

8. Damage

When you win a Roll Versus an opponent in combat you inflict Damage. After successfully hitting someone roll d6 and consult the Damage Charts on the inside front cover of this book. Reference your Damage Roll across the top row and the Weapon down the side. The result is the Damage inflicted and is deducted from your opponent's Stamina.

8.1 Double Damage

When striking a Mighty Blow (7.4) you double the amount of Stamina lost as a result of a Damage Roll.

8.2 Damage Modifiers

All modifiers that add bonuses to Damage, unless otherwise specified, modify the roll of the die, not the actual Damage inflicted. So, for instance, I have +1 to my Damage Roll and roll a 5 on the Sword entry. Due to my bonus I am counted as having rolled a 6 and inflict 8 Damage instead of 6.

8.3 Unusual Weapons

It is entirely acceptable to use existing Weapons to provide the Damage matrix of roughly equivalent Exotic Weapons, such as counting a Rapier as a Sword for Damage purposes. This does not preclude the possibility of making specific matrices for your inventions.

9. Armour

Armour offers a certain degree of protection to your soft and supple body. There are four levels of protection, vaguely defined, allowing you to assign whatever assortment of pots and pans you might be wearing to an appropriate level without too much bother. A target is considered to be Unarmoured, Lightly Armoured, Modestly Armoured, or Heavily Armoured. Each modifies Damage Rolls by 0, -1, -2 and -3 respectively, to a minimum of 1.

9.1 Armour Encumbrance

Armour takes up a number of item slots equal to twice its protective value. So Heavy Armour would use six slots, for example. See Section 10.2.

10. Encumbrance
You may carry twelve things without issue. On your character sheet are twelve spaces to write in the things you're lugging around with you.

10.1 Small Items
Some items are of inconsequential individual weight, like arrows, and only ever take up one slot (unless you have an awful lot of them). What constitutes a lot is up to your group to decide.

10.2 Large Items
Large items are anything you need both hands to hold. They take up two slots in your inventory (we recommend writing them at a jaunty angle to fill up the space). Armour has its own rules.

10.3 Retrieving Items in a Hurry
See Section 6.6. Note that having things near the top of your Inventory list is advantageous, so put things you'll rarely need in a hurry, like Armour and money, near the bottom. Pack your bags well!

10.4 Overburdened
If you find yourself carrying more than 12 items you suffer -4 to all rolls due to the inconvenient weight. If you are carrying 18 items or more you suffer -4 to all rolls, you can hardly move, and you count as Unawares (7.3) for anyone wanting to stab you.

> 10.4.1 Dropping Things in a Hurry. If you want to unburden yourself quickly roll 1d6. The result is how many slots of things you may carefully put down this Turn. At the GM's discretion you may roll 2d6 if you don't mind them getting broken or lost.

11. Getting Better

Life is learning and you cannot experience it without growing in some way. Your characters bend and change in response to their environment. When you successfully Test an Advanced Skill or Spell you stand to learn from it. Put a tick next to it on your character sheet.

11.1 How to Advance

The next time you have a chance to rest and reflect on your journey you may check to see what you have learned. Choose up to 3 Advanced Skills or Spells with a tick next to them. If you roll 2d6 OVER your current Skill Total (Advanced Skill/Spell + Skill) you may increase it by 1. When you have finished rolling, remove all ticks from your sheet.

> 11.1.1 12+ Advanced Skill. When an Advanced Skill has reached 12 you must roll a 12 followed by another 12 to improve it further. There is no upper limit to an Advanced Skill.

11.2 Training and Learning New Advanced Skills

It is also possible to improve your Advanced Skills or to learn new ones, though you must find someone willing to teach you. They must have a higher Skill Total (Advanced Skill/Spell + Skill) than you, and most likely require payment unless they are your fellow party member or already owe you a favour. Training takes 1 week plus 1 week per rank you already have in the Advanced Skill you are looking to improve. At the end of this time you get one chance at advancement. Failure means you just have to train harder. When learning new Advanced Skills you must Roll Under your Skill on 2d6 (precocious students are easier to teach) to gain your first point.

12. Advanced Skill Descriptions

In most cases the use of a Skill requires a straight Roll Under Skill Total (Advanced Skill + Skill). Situations where this isn't the case should be obvious.

The available Skills are not limited to those listed here. There should be rarer fare available for those who search for it or maybe a character just feels driven to learn the intricacies of farming or opera for some peculiar reason. You may notice some Skills in the Backgrounds section that don't have entries. Make those up.

Since the players don't ever have to waste time picking through the whole selection don't be afraid of expanding the list and making them more and more specific.

Acrobatics
Used for rolling, balancing, falling, jumping, etc.

Astrology
An essential Skill for anyone intent on travelling the stars. Can be used to identify stars and constellations, to gather hints on the destination of interdimensional portals, and to make star charts.

Awareness
Anything worth having is well hidden so one must look very carefully. Use this to spot traps, things normally hidden, or things out of the ordinary.

Climb
The usefulness of the ability to clamber up things cannot be overstated. Most climbs should be single rolls though longer or more difficult climbs may require multiple rolls. On these climbs consider requiring a number or total or repeated failures to fall off unless it is a particularly merciless ascent. The GM should use their discretion.

Crafting Skills
This includes any Skill you might think of that comes under the heading of arts and crafts. Blacksmithing, carpentry, painting, opera singing, anything like that. Roll Under the Skill if you want to do something that knowledge of this Skill would reasonably cover. A carpenter might be able to spot a weak bridge while a blacksmith could shoe a horse or an opera singer could identify an aria. Be flexible and reasonable.

Disguise
Covers the use of props to change your appearance. When in disguise you must Roll Under this when someone is liable to see through it. Opposed by Awareness when under scrutiny.

Etiquette
When making a good impression is important Roll Versus your host's Etiquette. Represents a mechanical understanding of social conduct and those who are better at it are more discerning.

Evaluate
Test this to get an idea of how much something is worth.

Fly
Use Fly much as you would Run. In normal situations this doesn't need testing, only in chases or high winds, maybe. Anyone attempting to Fly without this Skill must Test every Round to make sure they don't crash or lose control.

Golden Barge Pilot
Test this to navigate between the stars on a ship with golden mirror sails.

Healing
Used to stitch wounds and apply ointments, stop bleeding, slow poison and the like. Also used for stabilising dying people.

Languages
Represents relative competence in specific languages and would only need to be Tested if trying to understand something incredibly arcane or technical. It's assumed that once you have one point in a language you can understand it passably. You get one tick in a language for every month of intense tuition or complete submersion in it.

Locks
This allows a character to examine and open locks but does not detect traps. Roll Versus an imaginary locksmith whose Skill is somewhere between 6 and 12 with 6 being easy and 12 being very hard.

Mathmology
Use this to gain insight into angles, pressures, numbers, and other such arcane arts. You could, for instance, Test your Mathmology to get a good idea of the surface tension of a ball of inert plasmic goo or to find the fulcrum for tripping a giant.

Poison

You may Test this Skill during down time to create a single dose of poison. Pick which kind it is when you make it. This list is not exhaustive — more exotic ones may be available if you possess the knowledge and ingredients.

1D3	COMMON POISONS OF TROIKA
1	Causes anyone ingesting it to Test their Luck (or Skill for Enemies) or lose 4d6 Stamina.
2	Add 1 to all Damage Rolls while this is applied to piercing or edged Weapons. If you Roll a 1 for Damage the poison has worn off.
3	Causes anyone ingesting it to fall unconscious for 1d6 hours.

Ride

Everyone is assumed to have basic animal riding Skill, though anything more than trotting slowly requires some kind of roll to avoid trouble.

Run

When it matters how fast you are, or if you can reach somewhere in time, use this. A basic chase is an Roll Versus.

Second Sight

Use of this allows the detection of magic. On a successful Test you focus your inner eye and all sorcerous activity glows faintly for a moment.

Secret Signs

Used to identify marks, handshakes, code words, etc. of one specific society. You would, for example, be able to read the secret marks left on people's door posts by fellow hobos.

Sleight of Hand

Steal or hide small things. This is Tested only if someone is actively looking for them. A character may simply declare they are hiding something, only rolling this when the hiddenness is questioned.

Sneak

The art of remaining unseen. This is Tested only when someone or something is actively trying to detect you. The sneaker would Roll Versus the Awareness of those searching for them; anyone beating the sneaker's score detects them.

Strength

Used for lifting and breaking things. May also be used to grapple people if no grappling-appropriate Weapon Skill is possessed, though it counts for half rounded up.

Swim

Use this while swimming in dangerous waters, diving, holding your breath for long periods, and so on. If you have this Skill you don't need to roll it for normal conditions. Characters without it are assumed to not be able to swim and need to test Swimming every round they remain in the water or start Drowning (7.9). Receive a penalty to this Skill equal to half the number of item slots filled.

Tracking

Used to stalk prey and find tracks. When stalking a quarry this is treated as an opposed Roll Versus the opponent's Tracking or Sneaking.

Trapping

Use this to set and disarm traps. When setting traps Roll Under your Trapping Skill and describe how the trap is made with the materials at hand. When someone wishes to disarm a trap they must Roll Versus the original trap-setter's Trapping Skill. If the GM doesn't know what that number should be assume 6 to be pretty simple while 12 is incredibly hard. Scale it between those as appropriate.

Tunnel Fighting

You may use this Skill in place of your Weapon Skill while fighting in confined spaces where you would otherwise be unable to swing your Weapon about. You ignore all penalties the GM might associate with fighting in such a situation.

Weapon Fighting

Choose what general category of Weapons this covers when you take this Skill. Roll Versus during combat when using the appropriate method of assault. The GM is encouraged to allow Weapon categories to be broadly applicable, such as Glaive Fighting being equivalent to Polearm Fighting.

Other

If a Skill isn't listed here then make it up. Anything can be a Skill, from Jousting to Gambling to Eating. Skills are primarily used as flavour and the occasional fun instance where your incredibly specific and heretofore useless ability helps you and your friends out is priceless.

13. Items

13.1 If an item is not listed here assume it adds a bonus of +1 to rolls associated with it. Lockpicks, for instance, would add +1 to Lock rolls while a rope would add +1 to Climb, and so on.

13.2 Item bonuses only apply if you are trained in the Skill they are meant to enhance. Lockpicks only give their bonus if you know how to use lockpicks (have 1+ in Locks already).

13.3 An incomplete list of desirous things:

ASTROLOGICAL EQUIPMENT requires twenty minutes to set up and use but doesn't need to be outside. Consists of a ruby specular, charms against reciprocal observation, and complicated charts of the Spheres. Grants +1 to Astrology.

A BALE HOOK counts as a Knife for Damage and grants +1 on rolls to lift heavy objects.

THE BLUE STAR MAPS OF CORDA hold the secrets of travel between the Spheres. Every juncture in space and time can be found on its many square metred face if one is sufficiently educated in its use. Test Astrology to tell the precise destination of any portal.

AN EPOPT'S STAFF is a tool, an advert, and, in a pinch, a Weapon. In its head is set a CLOUDY RUBY, like a useless magnifying glass, which grants the user +1 Second Sight while peering through it.

A FUSIL is a long Weapon that looks like a rifle and can be used in melee as a Club. A Fusil holds 6 charges before the plasmic core needs replacing.

KNUCKLE DICE are made from the nimble, petal shaped knuckle bones of goblins and make excellent two sided dice.

A PISTOLET is a hand held energy Weapon. Holds enough energy for 8 shots.

PLASMIC CORES are crystalised starlight cast in metal. Or astral vapours captured in glass. Or maybe hard-ghosts? Whatever it is, it's pretty and used as a fuel source for exotic Weapons and reckless magicians. A PLASMIC CORE can be cracked open and huffed by a wizard in place of spending Stamina on a Spell. However, if an Oops! Table roll is called for the wizard has overdosed and drops dead, foaming at the mouth.

THE POCKET BAROMETER is part of a fashionable affectation for the metropolitan Troikan. Though the city has no discernible weather it is considered polite to check it intermittently and comment on the present clemency and hope for it to continue into the future. Examining its quartz face informs you of future weather with 5 in 6 accuracy.

POCKET GODS are little cloth puppets made in the image of numerous gods. If you whisper a secret to one and throw it away you regain 1 Luck.

RUBY LORGNETTES are collapsible spectacles made with ruby lenses that require a free hand to use. While wearing them your sight is impaired but you can see sorcerous activity clearly (+2 Second Sight).

SALT is the poor man's *SILVER*. Where *SILVER* kills the demonic and the dead *SALT* merely harms or bars.

SILVER is the star metal, the most untouched material fallen from the hump-backed sky. Weapons made from it may inflict Damage to creatures normally immune to material harm.

A *TEA SET* grants +1 to Etiquette when you have the time to sit down and make tea for those you are trying to impress.

THE VELARE, when inactive, looks like an ornate piece of costume jewellery, usually a brooch or a circlet. When active it produces a full body disguise on the wearer formed from hard-light. Grants +4 Disguise. Lasts for 24 hours before needing to be recharged with a *PLASMIC CORE.*

WITCH-HAIR ROPES are immune to manipulation via magical means.

A *YOKE* gives you +4 carry capacity while worn but you can't use your hands while wearing it.

14. Spells

To cast a Spell you must spend Stamina equal to the casting cost (the number in brackets) and Roll Under your Skill Total in the Spell you wish to cast. Double 1s always succeed. Double 6s always fail and require a roll on the Oops! Table.

Affix (3)

Cause a subject to be fixed in place. While they are so held they do not move, breathe, fall, perspire, acquire, or otherwise change. They are totally immune to harm, in fact. Lasts for 3 minutes.

Amity (4)

The College of Friends always sends out its Factotums on nights after Amity classes. Clearing out the bars and brothels of their drunken apprentices is tiring work. Use of this Spell causes the target to Test their Luck (or Skill for Enemies) or become very friendly towards the wizard, as though they were an old friend. They won't act irrationally, though, and if they were already a bit of a boor this might not change much.

Animate (2)

Cause inanimate objects to question their place. One object up to the size of a human baby may be caused to hop around and do whatever else the wizard wishes.

Assassin's Dagger (3)

Evocatively named but actually quite mundane. The wizard whispers to an object and that object then seeks out and vigorously and repeatedly bumps into the desired target. Obviously if you whisper to a poisoned dagger the result is one thing while doing it to a letter is another. Travels any distance and always arrives (eventually).

Assume Shape (4)

The wizard undergoes a distressing transformation into an inanimate object no larger than a piano and no smaller than a cup. Lasts until ended.

Astral Reach (1)

The Sorcerers of the Academy of Doors are most famous for this one Spell. With it they may reach through any portal and into another known receptacle. For example they might use it to reach through to a safe in their manse via their purse. This Spell only allows partial translocation—the wizard cannot fully or permanently enter.

Babble (2)
The wizard speaks nonsense while watching the intended target, causing their words to trip and confuse. This may be done under their breath and relatively subtly.

Banish Spirit (6)
The wizard explains, clearly, sternly, why it is impossible that the spirit could be here at this time. The spirit must Test its Luck (or Skill for Enemies) or be sent to somewhere less improbable.

Befuddle (1)
A wizard's touch can shake up someone's mind like a snow globe. The target makes all rolls at a -1 penalty until their head clears. Lasts for 3 minutes.

Blood Shroud (4)
Smear a small amount of a demon's blood on yourself to become completely invisible to them, even if you attack or speak to them, for 6 hours.

Breach (2)
The wizard's hands work elemental material as though it were soft clay. Fire, stone, goo, earth, fog, all of it behaves like clay under their touch. Lasts for 9 minutes.

Brittle Twigs (2)
You snap a twig or other brittle object to cause an injury in another. They must Test their Luck (or Skill for Enemies) or suffer a broken bone.

Callous Strike (1)
The Wizard-Knights are most famous for their remote combat whereby they swing their Silver Swords seemingly at nothing only for their opponents, many metres away, to be torn to tatters. This Spell can be used in place of a melee attack by Rolling Versus as normal and inflicting Damage according to the Weapon used. May only be used against targets within clear sight.

Coal Resolve (1)
This Spell turns one's heart into a burning ember of grief. Those under its effect are so consumed by grief that they are immune to mind controlling effects and the non-physical impact of pain. Lasts until the next rest.

Cockroach (5)
A popular Spell that turns troublesome folk into humiliated animals. The target must Test their Luck (or Skill for Enemies) or be turned into an insignificant creature of the wizard's choice. Lasts forever.

Cone of Air (2)

Creates a mysterious and specifically shaped cone of air focused on a touched target's head. They may continue to breathe the freshest of air for 12 minutes.

Darkness (3)

Summon a stationary, perfect sphere of darkness up to five metres from the wizard for up to 3 minutes.

Darksee (1)

The wizard reaches into their sockets and extricates their eyes. Thus freed, the dark void behind can see perfectly well in pitch blackness and suffer excruciating pain in light (-4 penalty to all rolls). Be careful not to lose those eyeballs as re-inserting them is the only way to end the Spell.

Diminish (2)

Cause something to Test its Luck (or Skill for Enemies) or reduce its size by half. Lasts 3 minutes.

Drown (4)

Cause a target's lungs to fill with water. They must Test their Luck (or Skill for Enemies). If they fail they start to Drown (7.9) and are incapacitated as water pours from their mouth. They may Test again once per Turn until they pass, at which point the Spell ends.

Earthquake (5)

The wizard hikes up their wizard robe and stomps their wizard feet. An area 30 metres around them suffers a massive earthquake. Everyone must Test their Luck (or Skill for Enemies) or fall through a crack in the earth, taking falling Damage and being stuck in a bloody great big hole (7.8.1). Buildings may be wrecked unless especially sturdy.

Ember (2)

A simple but effective summoning of fire. Flames the size of a small bonfire appear somewhere within 12 metres of the wizard. Once present there is no accounting for its actions.

Exchange Shape (5)

What looks like a hug is in fact fell wizardry! The wizard bumps into another and exchanges bodies. Lasts until the wizard chooses to end it but they must be within sight of their own body for this to happen.

Exorcism (1)

The Red Priests posit that all negative behaviour is a symptom of some level of possession, or at least direct influence, by the forces of Change, unwitting agents of Mass in need of healing. The wizard throws salt at their target and Rolls Versus the possessing spirit to cast it out. In the case of a Fumble the spirit is drawn into and possesses the wizard.

Explode (5)

So simple that it's arguably not even a Spell but rather a premeditated failure of catastrophic proportions. The wizard causes a one cubic metre object to explode and deal Damage to everyone within 24 metres depending on proximity. Those within 6 metres take Damage as a Gigantic Beast, within 12 as a Large Beast, 18 as a Modest Beast and 24 as a Small Beast.

Farseeing (2)

Endows the wizard with engorged, plate-like eyes that are able to see in minute detail for miles around but are unable to see anything up close. Lasts until ended.

Fear (1)

In the eyes of one poor target the wizard grows into a primal monster from the depths of their lizard brain. They attempt to flee, and if flight is impossible they curl up in a ball and whimper. They may Test their Luck (or Skill for Enemies) to resist the illusion.

Find (2)

When wizards lose their glasses they mumble to themselves until they turn up. The thing being sought must be a specific object, not a general category or type, and the direction is only given in terms of compass points.

Fire Bolt (1)

Shoot impressive flames from your fingertips, dealing Damage to one target within 20 metres.

Damage Roll➜	1	2	3	4	5	6	7+
Fire Bolt	3	3	5	7	9	12	16

Flash (3)

The wizard claps neatly and issues forth the light of a thousand suns from their hands. All within 20 metres must Test their Luck (or Skill for Enemies) or be blinded for 1d6 minutes.

Gills (3)

The wizard may permanently gift a touched subject with gills, replacing their usual breathing arrangement if they fail to Test their Luck (or Skill for Enemies). Useful for underwater excursions but less so when inflicted upon a chap in the middle of town. The wizard may end this at will.

Grow (2)

Cause an item to grow half its size again if it fails to Test its Luck (or Skill for Enemies). Lasts for 3 minutes.

Helping Hands (1)

Animate hands spring forth from an inanimate surface and perform any task the wizard requires but are limited to being rooted to the spot from which they sprang. They last until the wizard wills it or leaves the location.

Hurricane (5)

The wizard waves their hands in the air like they just don't care, which, being wizards, they likely don't. A mighty gust knocks everyone over within 30 metres who fails to Test their Luck (or Skill for Enemies), dealing 1d3 Damage and making an awful mess. Lasts for 10 minutes. Test Luck every Turn if not taking cover or else take further Damage.

Illusion (2 per viewer)

Those viewing this illusion may Test their Luck (or Skill for Enemies) to unveil the trickery. Lasts until the wizard leaves or falls asleep.

Invisibility (3)

The wizard turns flesh into refractive crystal sheets. It's very uncomfortable and you make a slight shish-ing sound as you move but are quite invisible and don't suffer from the usual limitations of illusions. Lasts for 3 minutes after which you noisily reform into dull and frustratingly opaque flesh.

Ironhand (3)

The common man does not appreciate exactly how close flesh and iron are when considered relative to, say, flesh and the smell of hot tea. With some slight convincing the wizard may cause a target's flesh to behave as though it had the desirable properties of metal. They get +1 Skill and immunity to modestly proportioned fires for 3 minutes.

Jolt (1)

The mischievous apprentice's favourite Spell, Jolt sends an arc of electricity from the wizard's outstretched hand towards a target. Ignores Armour.

Damage Roll→	1	2	3	4	5	6	7+
Jolt	2	2	3	3	5	7	9

Languages (1)
The wizard forms a mouth with their hands through which they can speak any language. They can simultaneously cup their other hand to their ear to understand them in return. Lasts for one conversation.

Leech (2)
The necromancer must place their hands on a living subject and allow their fingertips to transform into sucking apertures which drain the victim of blood. Deal 2d6 Damage to your victim and regain half as much Stamina.

Levitate (2)
Elevates the wizard or another on the backs of tiny invisible sprites who answer only to their summoner. May float about for 3 minutes.

Life Line (1)
Created by the Horizon Knights to enable them to take the fight to the Nothing, they would cast this on their squires and dive off the edge of creation. While this Spell lasts, the wizard's essential bodily functions are linked to another, thereby enabling them to breath or eat for the recipient. They need to breathe and eat for two, which makes it hard to do anything useful while linked. The Spell lasts for a day, until cancelled, or until the death of the linked person. Note if the linked person dies, starves, or is choked you suffer equally.

Light (1)
Create an ethereal orb of light that glows like a torch. Lasts 6 hours and can be extinguished at will.

Lock (1)
Magically lock an object. The object must have a lockable aspect to it but is now magically sealed. Permanent until undone or dismissed.

Mirror Selves (3)
In the minds of others the wizard appears to be, in fact, three wizards. All three perform the same actions in unison, offering attackers only a 1-in-3 chance of targeting the right wizard. Lasts for 12 minutes.

Natter (1)
As everyone knows, wizards are excellent ventriloquists, so good, in fact, that they can throw their voice inside another's mouth. They can target anyone within sight and transmit a short sentence.

Open (1)
The wizard chooses a reality wherein the lock was open all along. May be used to open any mundane door or container and counteract a Lock Spell.

Peace (2)

Open up the mind to universal love and cause two subjects to Test their Luck (or Skill for Enemies) or cease hostilities. They still defend themselves if attacked but at least appreciate the pettiness of it.

Poison (1)

When cast upon a liquid this Spell causes it to become deadly poison. The liquid deals 4 Damage if drunk and 1 Damage per Turn until the target successfully Tests their Luck (or Skill for Enemies). The liquid loses its potency after an hour.

Posthumous Vitality (5)

Necromancers, known for their social inadequacy, often find themselves having to make friends.

This Spell requires a fresh, or at least whole and lubricated, corpse. The wizard rolls 2d6 plus their Posthumous Vitality Skill Total and consults the following chart (13+ counts for an Advancement tick):

4-12	Nothing happens.
13-14	The vitality is clumsily applied, causing the body to explode messily. A new one must be found.
15-16	The creature is animated and lasts for 24 hours before literally falling to pieces.
17+	Perfect reanimation. The creature lasts until destroyed.

Presence (1)

This Spell creates the sense of being watched by a patriarchal figure. Some find it comforting, others, not so much.

Protection from Rain (1)

This Spell prevents the wizard from getting rained upon for one shower.

Purple Lens (1)

The recipient's eyes glow purple as they experience an alternative reality where people are kind, their surroundings are beautiful, their food is indulgent, and so on. This doesn't change the reality of things but it does make them more palatable. Lasts until they want it to end.

Quench (1)

Snuff a small flame with the wave of a hand.

Read Entrails (1)
The wizard can get the answer to one question from the entrails of a living creature. The size and importance of the creature influences the level of knowledge gained. Small, common animals are able to offer yes or no answers, oxen can predict things obtusely, lamassu may offer explicit and thorough advice.

Read Stars (1)
Rather than physical stars the wizard navigates by astral starlight that peeks through the veil. This Spell enables the wizard to get a reasonable sense of direction regardless of any obscuring factors.

See Through (1)
The wizard rubs a surface vigorously, making it translucent. Can penetrate up to 12 inches of material. Lead and Silver are immune.

Sentry (1)
The wizard plucks a bit of their mind out like candy floss and leaves it stuck to a wall somewhere. This psychic presence is invisible to the naked eye but extends the wizard's senses to that spot for the duration. While it lasts the wizard suffers -1 to all rolls due to the incredible confusion this generates. If the shard is discovered and harmed the wizard loses 2d6 Stamina due to the shock.

Shatter (3)
The wizard may wildly gesticulate at a brittle object no larger than an umbrella and cause it to shatter into a million pieces. Living targets may Test their Luck to avoid this unpleasant Spell.

Skeletal Counsel (3)
Necromancers often talk to skulls. Sometimes they talk back. Use of this Spell enables speaking with the dead, who answer one question per casting. Requires a skull.

Sleep (2)
The wizard convinces a target to forgo wakefulness for a time, causing them to sleep until woken unless they successfully Test their Luck. Remember: fighting is loud.

Slide Skywards (6)

Requires mirrors or other highly reflective surfaces. The wizard stands between two reflective surfaces so that they are infinitely repeated. They then step out from between them but as a different incidence of themselves. To those watching the wizard moves in the direction not seen and reappears between two mirrors elsewhere. If the location has been compromised the wizard arrives in a random mirrored location somewhere across the million crystal Spheres.

Starry Orb (4)

The wizard creates a 5th dimensional orb above their head. All intelligent beings looking at it must Test their Luck or marvel at it for 3 minutes.

Teleport (10)

The wizard or a target of their choosing may travel to any location within a single Sphere instantly. If unfamiliar with the location they must Test their Luck (or Skill for Enemies) or be thrown wildly off course to potentially devastating results.

Thought Vapour (1)

The wizard can cause their nose to exist in multiple alternative realities, travel through various Spheres, and enable the olfactory sensation of thought. Emotions, attitudes, and underlying feelings can be smelled. No words or images are formed, just impressions. Any strong odour causes this Spell to fail.

Thunder (2)

The wizard raises their arms and shouts something suitably ominous. All within 24 metres must Test their Luck (or Skill for Enemies) or be deafened by a riotous roll of thunder. Luck or no, they are mightily impressed.

Tongue Twister (2)

Beware! If a wizard screws their nose and twists their fingers at you then a Tongue Twister is coming your way. The target must Test their Luck (or Skill for Enemies) or have their tongue literally tied in knots. This requires some time and a fair bit of patience to disentangle.

Torpor (3)

Those who study the dead consider it necessary to develop a profound sympathy with their subject — how can you speak with the dead if you don't understand the dead? Torpor helps build post-mortem empathy by causing the necromancer to temporarily die. Bodily functions are halted, no food, water, or air is needed, and they are, by most vulgar definitions of the word, dead. The Spell lasts until ended by the wizard, who remains vaguely aware of their surroundings to the extent of being conscious of sound and movement but not of what is said or who is saying it. They still take Damage from bodily abuse while under the effect and can indeed become irretrievably dead.

True Seeing (3)

The wizard focuses their sight on the unambiguous truth of matter, enabling them to see through illusions for the next 10 minutes.

Undo (double cost of original Spell)

The wizard disentangles a Spell from this instance of reality. To do so they must Roll Versus the original casting if disentanglement is possible at all.

Ward (1)

A handy Spell only requiring the flick of a wrist. In response to being fired upon the wizard may cast this Spell to cause the missile to be deflected.

Wall of Power (2)

What they call a wall is in fact a dome, but wizards always have worked in mysterious ways. The wall is a shimmering bubble that causes 1d6 Damage when touched. Nothing may pass without the wizard's permission (it is recommended that they remember to allow air). Lasts for 12 minutes.

Web (2)

Whether this is opening a portal to the plane of slime or channelling the sprites of sickness, all can agree that it is quite disgusting. The wizard blows forth the "web" from their nose and all in a cone extending 12 metres in front of the wizard are trapped unless they Test their Luck (or Skill for Enemies). Each Turn anything passing through or out of it must repeat the Test or become stuck. Dries up after 12 rounds.

Zed (?)

No one knows what this does but everyone who has cast it disappears instantly, never to be seen again.

15. Enemies
Enemies that characters encounter are not like them—they are simpler machines that produce similar results.

15.1 Enemy Skill is Not Like Character Skill
Enemy Skill covers everything they lack, including Advanced Skills and Luck. They use the same number to climb a rope as to hit or cast a Spell.

15.1.2 Enemy Spells do not cost Stamina.

15.1.2 Enemies do not spend Luck. They don't have a Luck score and instead Roll Versus their Skill, which never diminishes. They also may not Test their Luck to gain an advantage for themselves in combat, such as testing Luck to increase Damage.

15.2 Why the Stamina Disparity?
The Stamina of enemies tends towards lower numbers than characters. This is to speed battles along and to make it somewhat fairer on the characters who must spend Stamina for their magic. Note that the combat rules and Damage have been balanced in such a way that a goblin is a threat no matter how much Stamina it has.

15.3 Initiative is Different for Enemies
While all characters contribute two Initiative Tokens each, enemies have their own specific totals. These are all the same colour and are added to the Initiative Stack and drawn similarly to the characters' Initiative Tokens. When an Enemy Token is drawn the GM may use it to activate and take a Turn with any enemy present.

There is no limit to the number of times a single enemy may act in a Round—indeed you could have one enemy perform all actions drawn. This does not represent speed so much as it represents commitment to action while others stall or perform minor tasks (5.5).

EXAMPLE: A lizard-man and a goblin are fighting the characters, both of which are contributing to the Initiative Stack. When an enemy Initiative Token is drawn the GM may declare that either one of them is acting.

15.4 Armour is the Same
Rather than have varying types of Armour enemies just have a number. This is treated exactly the same as the numbers associated with character Armour and represents physical protection, speed, incorporeality, etc.

15.5 Mien
If you have a plan for the enemies' attitude then go with that. Otherwise Roll to see how they appear when meeting the group. Use this as inspiration when playing them and to help avoid falling into routine hostility.

Bestiary
Alzabo

Skill 10
Stamina 21
Initiative 4
Armour 1
Damage as Large Beast

MIEN	
1	Hungry
2	Confused
3	Protective
4	Patient
5	Watchful
6	Evasive

The red furred ghoul-bear, which at its shoulder stands as tall as a horse, would be a frightful creature for no other reason than its immediate physical impression. The Alzabo can produce — for it is not truly mimicking, rather recalling — the exact sound of any creature it has ever eaten. Crying out in the night, it draws its prey from safety, typically by imitating a recently eaten family member and calling to its children or parents. Even if the devoured is human and those listening know that it's not truly them, the sound of a daughter you know to be dead tapping at your cottage door and begging to be let in from the cold is more than most can bear.

Boggart

Skill 6
Stamina 9
Initiative 2
Armour 0
Damage as Weapon or Modest Beast

MIEN	
1	Belligerent
2	Obstinate
3	Petulant
4	Insolent
5	Sullen
6	Smug

You could be forgiven for thinking a boggart was a rangy man with an exceedingly bristly beard, but no, once upon a time it sprung fully formed from a hole and has been ungrateful and ill prepared for everything since. They rarely travel far from their birth hole although there is no pixie compulsion to do so, it's more a point of principle and lack of imagination on their part. They can, if provoked, be violent in the defence of the land which they consider to be theirs but they are prideful, stupid, and easily tricked.

Bonshad

Skill 12
Stamina 20
Initiative 3
Armour 2
Damage as Gigantic Beast

MIEN	
1	Wrathful
2	Virulent
3	Spiteful
4	Nauseated
5	Acquisitive
6	Imperious

The Bonshad is the source of an amusing piece of trivia amongst diabolists. While it is well known that the Bonshads know the method of creating the Elixir of Shazmazm it is less well known (at least amongst impatient apprentices) that *The 17th Incantation of Ignis Baxter: Bring Up What Bonshad Come* contains a typo in the 5th chorus. You can imagine the embarrassment this would have caused Master Baxter had he not been tragically caught up in the Oblation Wars soon after completing his seminal work. Regardless, calling up this hook-beaked betentacled fiend without the reformed texts sees one dragged off to the bottom of the Demon Sea to work their curious mines. What a lark!

Cyclops

Skill 9
Stamina 14
Initiative 3
Armour 2
Damage as Large Beast

MIEN	
1	Tearful
2	Depressed
3	Melancholic
4	Sombre
5	Resigned
6	Mercurial

Once upon a time a nation of man asked one of the Aeons to grant them the power of immortality and foresight. The Aeons, being an arbitrary bunch, took one eye from each as fair exchange. The men found that their foresight was indeed present but extended only to knowledge of their eventual deaths by accident or violence. Feeling positively monkey-pawed they agreed to go their separate ways and to never speak of it again.

Special

When a cyclops is given Initiative it may draw the next three Initiatives in order, thus granting them knowledge of who is going next. They know when and how they die and this might not be it.

Dolm

Skill 7
Stamina 21
Initiative 2
Armour 1
Damage as Large Beast

	MIEN
1	Unperturbed
2	Detached
3	Tranquil
4	Tired
5	Curious
6	Perturbed

Somewhere beneath the earth they sit suspended in their cavities, peacefully contemplating the movements of the surface world. A witness to their inter-crevice ambling would see a large, saggy-skinned humanoid with soulful grey eyes staggering as though carrying a heavy basin of water. The dolm never stops growing, as far as anyone can tell, and the oldest and wisest of their sort can tower above a typical townhouse while still being able to squeeze themselves under the door.

Special

A dolm can compress itself to fit in any crack through which they can pass their eyes. These, unlike the rest of them, never grow beyond the size of a typical human eye.

Donestre

Skill 9
Stamina 14
Initiative 3
Armour 0
Damage as Modest Beast

	MIEN
1	Gregarious
2	Urbane
3	Exhilarated
4	Impassioned
5	Shameful
6	Grieving

There is a certain creature of a solitary nature with a huge feline head topped with a gentle flowing mane, they glitter with numinous light and speak the language of all thinking beings. They dazzle travellers with knowledge of their past and the places they have been and are going. Indeed their knowledge seems deep, broad, and generously given. Their hunger for company is an honest one, their enthusiasm is endless, but they can't control themselves. As the conversation flows they become more and more fervent until their passion ignites and they devour their companion up to the neck. They continue to sadly converse with the head for a time before shamefully burying it and moving on.

Drock

Skill 6
Stamina 13
Initiative 2
Armour 0
Damage as Small Beast

	MIEN
1	Happy
2	Contemplative
3	Hungry
4	Tired
5	Unhappy
6	Confused

Dwarfs are creatures of purpose; they set their minds on a course and follow it until they finish or run aground. Occasionally a Dwarf is forcibly prevented from finishing an otherwise promising project, possibly by dropping dead at an inopportune moment; it happens. Usually this is a sad but inconsequential occasion, however sometimes it happens while they pursue the highest art a Dwarf can engage in: the creation of a new Dwarf. These creatures of raw surfaces, untreated stucco, brass armature, and soggy wet clay have a blind, unquenchable hunger to be finished by a virtuosic hand.

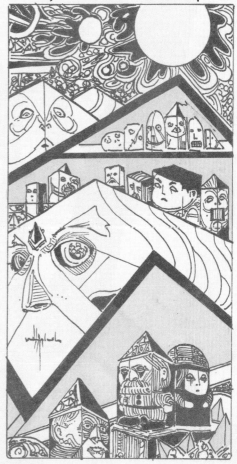

Dragon

Skill 16
Stamina 32
Initiative 8
Armour 4
Damage as Gigantic Beast

	MIEN
1	Sleeping
2	"Playful"
3	Hungry
4	Quizzical
5	Aggressive
6	Paranoid

Dragons are creatures of hyper-light, unburdened by base matter, able to soar across the dark sea of sky between worlds. Since their spirits are immortal and illuminated by the black-suns they may, and often do, indulge in base activities such as wanton slaughter, accumulating needless wealth, and plumbing the depths of forbidden knowledge. They do this because they know that nothing of these wicked Spheres can harm them or their objective spiritual and physical perfection.

Special

Once per Round they may douse a 24 foot area in beautiful Dragon-Fire. Everyone in the area is automatically hit but may Test their Luck to reduce the Damage Roll by 1.

Damage Roll➜	1	2	3	4	5	6	7+
Dragon-Fire	6	8	12	16	18	24	36

Dragons are immune to high temperatures, including Dragon-Fire.

Ekodat

Skill 8
Stamina 43
Initiative 3
Armour 2
Damage as Spear

	MIEN
1	Dormant
2	Stationary
3	Unstable
4	Probing
5	Tentative
6	Cautious

The Ekodat is a series of crystalline protrusions emanating from a clouded crystal core. These "tentacles" don't move; instead they grow rapidly through the air like roots. Natural philosophers have been back and forth about the categorisation of the Ekodat. While all agree it is a chimera of mineral and some other substance they cannot confirm the matter of the other. The popular attitude is that it is a divine emanation caught and refracted in some unusually dense crystal matrix, causing what would otherwise be an angelic visitation to become a mineralogical hazard.

Special

The tentacles remain after an attack. When an individual is successfully injured by the Ekodat they are immediately attacked again by the sudden growth of additional spurs brought on by the sufusion of vital fluids.

Feathered Folk

Skill 7
Stamina 6
Initiative 2
Armour 0
Damage as Bow

	MIEN
1	Pious
2	Sincere
3	Beatific
4	Rapt
5	Abstracted
6	Doubting

Profoundly religious though unfocused. Their civilisation worshiped the Egg of Time, which sat at the heart of their temple city on their holy mountain, until the day the Egg cracked and the god that leaped forth instantly shattered into a trillion shards of glass that flew off into the cosmos. Since then they have been eager to join any religion founded after that point, believing it to be a shard of the Born God.

Goblin

Skill 5
Stamina 6
Initiative 1
Armour 1
Damage as Weapon

	MIEN
1	Curious
2	Dismissive
3	Preoccupied
4	Gossipy
5	Overly Friendly
6	Paranoid

Goblins are the vanguard of civilisation. The moment a Sphere bobs to the surface the goblins creep out of the nooks and crannies to start expanding their labyrinth. Left to their own devices they eventually tame and cover every surface in walls and hedges and tunnels and steel and whatever else is in goblin-vogue, though more usually they are distracted with an accidentally awakened evil, or recalled by the Goblin King, or cut off from the centre of the labyrinth and turned feral to live in the man-cities. A most terrible fate. Better to bury their labyrinths and leave.

Gremlin

Skill 3
Stamina 4
Initiative 3
Armour 0
Damage as Small Beast

MIEN	
1	Inveigling
2	Fearful
3	Fearful
4	Aggressive
5	Aggressive
6	Fake Inveigling (Aggressive)

Vicious little creatures dressed in potato sacks they stole from an old mother's cupboards. When you see footprints in the pie crust it's time to call the Gremlin Catcher because where there's one there's a hundred and underneath your home is a veritable maze of warrens stretching off to gods know where.

No proven link between the gremlins' habit of appearing seemingly everywhere and the goblins' interdimensional labyrinth have been made but fingers are firmly pointed.

Harpy

Skill 8
Stamina 12
Initiative 3
Armour 0
Damage as Modest Beast

MIEN	
1	Spiteful
2	Malicious
3	Cruel
4	Hateful
5	Vicious
6	Barbaric

Immortal creatures of bitterness and spite, they look like vultures with human heads and unusually large claws. Their immortal nature precludes the need to eat yet they hunt mercilessly, most usually by lifting their quarry up into the sky and dropping them after spending some time verbally tormenting them. A greater pleasure still is when their victims survive the fall, whereupon they descend and eat the exposed sweetmeats and cackle with their mouths full. Altogether a reprehensible blight on creation.

Special

Harpies are natural sorcerers, each knowing Read Entrails and any other Spells you might deem appropriate.

Khaibit

Skill 9
Stamina 10
Armour 1
Initiative 3
Damage as Weapon

MIEN	
1	Austere
2	Bemused
3	Ecstatic
4	Bored
5	Impassive
6	Arresting

The Shadow Exultants make up the bulk of the Autarch's lower nobility, being the handmaids and officers filling out attendance at highborn social events. Each one possesses an uncanny resemblance to one Exultant or other, blood of their very blood as they are. They live in hope that their clone-parent dies and passes their Exultancy on to them but it is far more likely that they are at some point harvested for their life-extending component parts. Such is the *noblesse oblige*.

Knight of the Road

Skill 7
Stamina 7
Initiative 2
Armour 1
Damage as Weapon

MIEN	
1	Curious
2	Wary
3	Drunk
4	Rowdy
5	Predatory
6	Friendly

Contrary to what the farmers tell you the life of a vagabond is not an easy one. First you must find a road, but not a quiet road or else you'll wait for weeks without a client, nor should it be too busy or else you'll no sooner have belayed the first about the bonce before another comes along and interrupts your exchange. After all that you go back to your camp in the woods to sleep on the filthy ground and eat your meagre meals. Farmers should have more respect for a hard day's work.

Living Dead

Skill 6
Stamina 12
Initiative 1
Armour 0
Damage as Weapon or Modest Beast

MIEN	
1	Oblivious
2	Pondering
3	Distracted
4	Hungry
5	Aggressive
6	Distressed

The definition of 'dead' varies from place to place. In some Spheres you might be considered dead when unconscious or still living until buried. Now consider the ambulatory deceased and the definition is even more nebulous and near the point of irrelevance. Let's just say they have a fluid vitality.

Special
They take double Damage from Silver.

Lizard-Man

Skill 8
Stamina 8
Initiative 2
Armour 2
Damage as Weapon or Modest Beast

MIEN	
1	Severe
2	Hostile
3	Suspicious
4	Intolerant
5	Threatening
6	Inquisitive

Imagine a large man but this man is a crocodile. Stand him on his hind legs, yank his head into a civilised position, shorten his snout, and give him some short horns and a large Weapon. This is a lizard-man, a preternaturally militaristic race who spontaneously regiment themselves from the moment they goose-step their way out of the egg. Their only social structure and interest is the army, making them excruciatingly dull dinner guests.

Loathsome Wurm That Will Consume The Sun

Skill 12
Stamina 46
Initiative 7
Armour 3
Damage as Gigantic Beast

	MIEN
1	Tormented
2	Writhing
3	Envious
4	Phlegmatic
5	Rancorous
6	Malevolent

Once upon a distant time the gods banded together to mould the dripping flesh of the Monad into all the creatures of the earth. One Divine Architect, sneaky, lazy, or mad, consistently came up short on their daily quota of flesh-given-shape. At this point an exceptional storyteller would usually improvise a series of didactic vignettes of gods or animals asking why the god's work was lacking until finally the god revealed that they were saving scraps to create the Loathsome Wurm. The Thief-God was usually punished and their mad unfinished creature confined to the veins of the earth since destroying either was beyond the scope of their siblings' combined godly might. A trite story about the permanence of evil, but a popular and partially true tale.

In reality the Loathsome Wurm is the width of an elephant, with great tusks and grinding scales. Its unfinished, infinite body coils back into the depths and it can surely level the sunlit world were it not confined to the darkness from which it stares. If one listens closely at the thresholds of caves they may hear its whispers and promises. Treasures thrown down pits and left in cave mouths temporarily silence it.

Special

If killed, the stub of the creature's neck can be descended and used as an entry to the Primary Underworld. The Wurm reforms in 5,125 years.

Man-Beast

Skill 8
Stamina 11
Initiative 2
Armour 1
Damage as Fusil or Modest Beast

	MIEN
1	Heedful
2	Observing
3	Watchful
4	Questioning
5	Challenging
6	Aggressive

The Autarchs couldn't rely on the aristocracy for delicate or controversial matters; even for thoroughly mundane requests they were worshipful in word and recalcitrant in action and so towards the beginning of their reign an Autarch had their vizier fabricate armies of beastly chimera, utterly loyal to the Phoenix Throne, obeying orders to the letter unto death.

The man-beasts are far from mindless, rather they never question their lot in life, being unable to comprehend an alternative existence. Indeed, you might find man-beast guards still defending doorways to caches of Weapons and treasure the Autarchs are known to have hidden away for times of trouble, vigilant as a sleepless, incorruptible watchdog.

Manticore

Skill 12
Stamina 18
Initiative 5
Armour 3
Damage as Large Beast

	MIEN
1	Lazy
2	Bored
3	Hungry
4	Busy
5	Aggressive
6	Bored and Aggressive

Manticores are rarely encountered outside of their homes, which they tend to construct on mountain sides far out of reach of the common folk. The servants that attend them are kidnapped travellers plucked from the backs of wagons or dragged from their beds during the night.

If you have been hired by a patron to retrieve a stolen son from a manticore's manse be sure to take some books. They are inveterate culture fiends and love nothing more than having new literature for the help to read to them.

Special

If a manticore strikes the same person twice in one Round they have been hit by the creature's tail. They must Test their Luck (or Skill for Enemies) or become paralysed for 2d6 minutes.

Notule

Skill 9
Stamina 3
Armour 3
Initiative 3
Damage as Large Beast

MIEN	
1	Dormant
2	Probing
3	Flighty
4	Recoiling
5	Aggressive
6	Intent

A star-creature, sometimes caught roosting in the rigging of golden barges, formless, freezing to the touch, and valued for its utility as a tool of murder. By utilizing only the smallest bit of physical remains a knowledgeable sorcerer may set the creature hunting. It flies by night until reaching the intended victim, whereupon it envelops them, suffocating and freezing the target all at once and leaving a relatively unmarked corpse before sluggishly returning home to enjoy its newfound warmth.

Special

Anyone successfully hit by a notule must Test their Luck (or Skill for Enemies) or start to Drown. The notule wraps itself around their face and begins to suffocate them.

Ogre

Skill 9
Stamina 18
Initiative 3
Armour 1
Damage as Weapon or Large Beast

MIEN	
1	Smug
2	Generous
3	Covetous
4	Gregarious
5	Duplicitous
6	Offensive

The ogre is a phenomenon common across the universe. A child is born with a scowl on their face and a corded knot where their heart should be. They won't play with the other children, preferring to steal their toys and break them in privacy. As they age they become worse, larger, severe, and monstrous. The scowl never leaves their face, and they take no sincere joy in anything other than the acquisition of wealth and the suffering of others. Some cultures drive them into the woods and mountains to live out their days somewhat harmlessly, whereas in others they are rewarded. Their complete lack of shame and willingness to do anything in pursuit of their selfish goals makes them well suited for certain societies; an ogre governor, magnate, or baronet is a sadly common occurrence.

Orc

Skill 7
Stamina 8
Initiative 2
Armour 0
Damage as Weapon

	MIEN
1	Industrious
2	Confused
3	Homesick
4	Angry
5	Frustrated
6	Violent

The classical colleges of magic consider the orc to be an educational hazard. All young wizards will have seen posters in the common room warning of the dangers of unprotected sorcery, "Remember your wards!" "1 in 8 sorcerers know someone who has been affected by orcs!" and so on. As for the orcs themselves, well, who can blame them for their attitude? Being summoned across the cosmos by adolescent wizards is a distressing situation in which to find oneself.

Owl

Skill 4
Stamina 4
Armour 0
Initiative 1
Damage as Small Beast

	MIEN
1	Curious
2	Watchful
3	Aggressive
4	Hungry
5	Guarded
6	Defensive

The rooftops of Troika are crenelated by owls. They watch the streets with dumb spite, waiting for a vole, a rat, or an errant, fat finger to come to their attention. They swoop after it, followed by other owls blindly responding to the motion. Together they descend like a rabid flock of razor sharp gulls blindly grasping. A perennial pest that the citizens of Troika are morbidly proud of tolerating.

Parchment Witch

Skill 8
Stamina 14
Initiative 2
Armour 1
Damage as Weapon

MIEN	
1	Admiring
2	Infatuated
3	Obsessed
4	Paranoid
5	Skulking
6	Violent

Parchment Witches are an unusual breed of living dead both for having usually chosen the state of their own volition and for their staunch denial of it. They cover their rotting skin in a layer of leather, vellum, or, if no other option is available, paper. They then paint it, decorate it, and top it with a wig, thus completing the illusion. The most talented can walk among us and we'd never know it. The only tell-tale signs of a Parchment Witch among you would be the distinct smell of leather rendering in the house next door and the disappearance of a few handsome townspeople.

Special
Parchment Witches have 5 Spells rolled randomly or chosen ahead of time.

They take double Damage from Silver.

If given suitable time and supplies the Witch can completely change their appearance. They can also use the skin of another person to impersonate them for a week after which time it starts to rot.

Piscean

Skill 3
Stamina 6
Initiative 2
Armour 0
Damage as Modest Beast

MIEN	
1	Mewling
2	Childish
3	Playful
4	Mischievous
5	Hungry
6	Starving

Legs of a man, torso and tail of a fish. They break into granaries, batter the nightguards with their blubbery tails, stuff their bellies full of feed, and run off into the night to digest in a local lake. They are menaces!

Special
If they incapacitate a party member all able Pisceans descend on them and eat all their Provisions. Each consumes one per Turn.

Night Pig

Skill 7
Stamina 14
Initiative 2
Armour 0
Damage as Modest Beast

MIEN	
1	Sinister
2	Suspicious
3	Unreal
4	Inquisitive
5	Shameful
6	Cowardly

There are those witches that don the skin of a pig and walk abroad amongst their sleeping neighbours. Through the power imbued by that most sinister animal they rub themselves against the exteriors of houses and snuffle at their hedges, thereby ensorcelling the household's wealth to them. As the night goes on they grow increasingly fat, limited only by their greed. When they return home and remove their pig cape all the treasure they have stolen tumbles out. For this reason it's wise to demand answers from any pig you see out at night. Their intentions are never good.

Salamander

Skill 8
Stamina 16
Initiative 3
Armour 3
Damage as Large Beast

MIEN	
1	Convulsing
2	Expanding
3	Retracting
4	Surging
5	Revolving
6	Blooming

A star creature that sailors are accustomed to removing from their golden ships like terrestrial barnacles. They are attracted to the heat of the sails and interfere with their correct operation if not dealt with. When removed they are low and squat, so dark as to force your eyes to run off them, so hot that you can feel it from across a room. They move like tar, slow then fast, able to expand themselves to attack, in the moment looking like a quickly blooming rose. Even fatalistic golden sailors are careful when poking at shadows.

Separator

Skill 9
Stamina 12
Initiative 2
Armour 0
Damage as Medium Beast

	Mien
1	Uncanny
2	Hagridden
3	Withdrawn
4	Unassuming
5	Ravenous
6	Cruel

In an infinite universe there are infinite witches, amongst which is a rich spectrum of awfulness. Separators are some of the foulest. They live like normal people by day but by night feed their sorcery through teratic transformations. Sat in their home, their bodies pull away at the breastbone, tongues lengthen and hang to the ground, and wings sprout from their spinal columns. They fly invisibly in search of sleeping victims so as to force their tongues down their gullets to feast upon the innards. Their victims awaken mysteriously sick while the witch remains healthy and young.

Special
Sleeping victims lose 1d6 permanent Stamina daily unless magically restored.

By day they are indistinguishable from a normal person. By night the flying portion is invisible at will, only visible through Second Sight or magic. Destroying their dormant home-body traps them in their flying aspect.

Sympathy Serpent

Skill 5
Stamina 6
Initiative 2
Armour 0
Damage as Small Beast

	Mien
1	Shy
2	Friendly
3	Sympathetic
4	Fearful
5	Sad
6	Inconsolable

Dark, thick as a man's thigh, and as long as three destriers, they crush their prey as you'd expect such a snake to do but their hunting style is idiosyncratic: they do not wrestle with their quarry but offer a gentle embrace, telling them it's okay to let go, they're here now. Together prey and predator mourn the crushing awfulness of reality as one swallows the other whole.

Special
Sleeping or unsuspecting targets must Test their Luck (or Skill for Enemies) or be paralysed with misery and allow the serpent to quietly eat them.

Thinking Engine

Skill 8
Stamina 14
Initiative 2
Armour 1
Damage as Weapon

	MIEN
1	Absent Minded
2	Distracted
3	Enthusiastic
4	Maudlin
5	Sentimental
6	Engrossed

Built in the time of the First Empire, commissioned by the will of the Other Lords to pilot the golden ships of their cosmic civilisation. Each one is unfathomably ancient but by design or fault they don't remember more than a lifetime's worth of existence. We think of them in their common form of bakelite and chrome androids but their variety is a result of the chthonic imagination of the Other Lords and endless in its diversity. Most have been broken over their lifetimes and replaced their parts, some with new mechanical contrivances and others with organic flesh. Some have lost their original form altogether and walk the earth as flesh while others are large and hollow, waiting for an operator with dead knowledge.

Tiger

Skill 8
Stamina 12
Initiative 2
Armour 0
Damage as Large Beast

	MIEN
1	Playful
2	Stalking
3	Hungry
4	Tired
5	Austere
6	Aggressive

It is common knowledge that all tigers come from the Palace of Tigers. You may see one in a jungle somewhere and think they are at home, maybe they are even raising kittens and leading rich full tiger lives, but they are as alien to that forest as you or I, and the kittens are invariably stolen from lesser cats. They were born to leisure, to stalk fat little coati in palatial gardens, and to bask in crystal solariums. Take pity on these angry animals for they are lost and not used to your rude ways.

Tower Wizard

Skill 10
Stamina 12
Initiative 3
Armour 0
Damage as Weapon

MIEN	
1	Offensive
2	Confused
3	Friendly
4	Suspicious
5	Inappropriate
6	Transgressive

The majority of sorcery enthusiasts are either members of a college or well respected freelance lecturers with a nice manse in a seaside town, esteemed members of society who buy their groceries the same as us. However, when people think "wizard" they most likely go straight to the tower wizards, those feral old men who have given up all pretence of civility and fled to the wilderness. There they build their eponymous towers to work on unpleasant projects and terrorise the neighbourhood. They give magic a bad name.

Special

The Tower Wizard has access to Jolt or Ember and 4 other Spells rolled randomly or chosen ahead of time.

Troll

Skill 7
Stamina 12
Initiative 1
Armour 2
Damage as Weapon

MIEN	
1	Rude
2	Standoffish
3	Spiteful
4	Disrespectful
5	Sarcastic
6	Sullen

Trolls are ill-tempered creatures often spied leaning on a pike in the town square, gabbing with other guards while taking the occasional break to shout at a child, or tripping up an old lady. You'd think they'd stop hiring them.

Special

Trolls regenerate 1 Stamina every time they hold the Initiative. They also regenerate back from anything other than decapitation or fire.

Ven

Skill 8
Stamina 8
Initiative 2
Armour 2
Damage as Super Weapon

	MIEN
1	Frustrated
2	Scared
3	Curious
4	Fascinated
5	Quixotic
6	Depressed

The million Spheres have not been counted, it's just understood that there are a lot — countless by every useful standard. Eventually, in a future further from now than the birth of the Monad is from here, the hump-backed sky will fold in on itself and one crystal Sphere will remain. On that Sphere will be the last culture, the Ven, pale-skinned, dressed in rubber and peaked caps, spending the time left before the Monad rests in obscure and pointless pursuits. Their arts can do anything but prevent the End of All Things. Some amongst their people, not content to wait, fling themselves and some small portion of their arts back through time to live in a more vigorous era. There they try to achieve some imitation of their old lives, setting themselves up as demi-gods and tyrants obsessed with preventing the future they fled.

Zoanthrop

Skill 7
Stamina 12
Initiative 2
Armour 0
Damage as Modest Beast

	MIEN
1	Playful
2	Stalking
3	Hungry
4	Tired
5	Plagued by Thought
6	Aggressive

In the reign of the 35th Autarch it became fashionable to be seen as in-touch with the natural world. One could often witness Exultants abstaining from artificial cloth, conspicuously forgoing their flyers on shorter journeys, and walking barefoot through their palaces whilst their servants laid down petals in their path. This trend escalated until the more desperate social climbers ultimately committed to having their prefrontal cortexes partially removed in the pursuit of the greatest animal verisimilitude. While the results were undeniable, it prevented participation in even the most basic functions of state. The Autarch applauded their commitment but tastes soon moved on.

16. The Blancmange & Thistle
An Introductory Adventure

The Blancmange & Thistle is an extravagant hotel cast in gold and chrome. Chandeliers, ironwork, thick colourful mismatched carpets, paintings of every style, taste and era, guests in nooks buried in deep chairs seemingly built for them, mandrills everywhere, the smell of brass polish and artificial cherry in the air.

The characters arrive looking for suitably glamorous accommodation for their first few days in the city of Troika. The concierge informs the party that they are hosting their annual Feast of the Chiliarch on the roof and as a result there is unfortunately only one room on the 6TH FLOOR left and that they "simply must attend the party" and that it's "a positive delight to have you." In a fit of politeness you all agree to share the remaining room. Take a moment to allow the characters to consider their bedmates and deliver their hellos.

The concierge gives one character the small SILVER ROOM KEY on a chain too small for any neck and too large for any wrist. Have the player mark this in their Inventory.

According to the illuminated glass map of the hotel standing prominently in the foyer you have two choices in your ascent, being the Lift or the Stairs. Canny players might consider descending through the roof but anyone caught climbing the facade or rudely flying directly into the party is rebuffed by 2d6 MANDRILL GUARDS nesting in the crevices.

At every encounter the party has the option of continuing via the stairway or the lift to the 6TH FLOOR.

MANDRILL GUARD SKILL: 5 STAMINA: 10 INITIATIVE: 2
   BITE & CLAW as Modest Beast.
   LITTLE BLUE PADDED BUCKSKIN JACKET.
   SMALL SWORD.
   TINY CROSSBOW (as Crossbow with -1 to Damage Rolls).

How can I insert The Blancmange & Thistle into my game?

The Blancmange & Thistle can be placed anywhere though it is best suited to metropolitan areas prone to bouts of exoticism. If you have no existing game to put it in you should start right here with the characters arriving at the front desk, forced together by happenstance.

This place is dangerous, what if someone dies?

Have them create a new character and introduce them at the next floor. Hello new friend!

I don't know what's going on!

None of us do. Ride it out and see what happens! You can apply meaning and history to everything in your next session in light of the events of the first. Encourage the players to connect the dots for you.

Where's the bar?

Through a door to the side of the front desk, labelled with a colour-shifting neon garlic bulb. Stairs lead to a basement where you may buy a dizzying variety of exotic pickled vegetables. The only alcohol they sell is a clear herbal liqueur served in snifter glasses. The barman is ancient and deaf but the selection is so limited he can usually guess correctly. The music sounds like several lions roaring at the bottom of a well while someone plays the tuba energetically. The few guests here are gathering up their fireworks and preparing to leave for whichever Feast of the Chiliarch they're attending.

The Lift: Ground Floor

The lift is summoned with a wire cord set in the wall which issues a rapid series of clatters when yanked, like porcelain thrown in a sink. The lift doors are chromed, allowing the party a good look at themselves before the lift arrives. In a short moment its chrome doors open and two persons covered entirely in interlocking metal plates step out in unison and head towards the exit of the hotel.

Inside the lift is an ironwork cage, a thick green carpet floor that you sink several inches into, and a small chandelier with phosphore bulbs which brush against tall characters' heads. The walls of the lift shaft are painted at every floor and in between with gradients of colour. There are no floor numbers, only distinct tones that get lighter as you ascend.

There is a **tiny mandrill** in a tiny red suit operating an arcane set of controls for the lift. **The mandrill** can't speak but it understands people perfectly well and takes them to their floor when asked or upon being shown the proper ROOM KEY. **The mandrill** always opens the doors for guests at floors they wish to enter or exit, regardless of objections, though it may be distracted with bribes of food.

The lift moves slowly and generates a hum that is registered in the teeth.

MANDRILL LIFT ATTENDANT *SKILL:* **5** *STAMINA:* **10** *INITIATIVE:* **2**
BITE & CLAW as Modest Beast.

1ˢᵗ Floor Passenger: The Old Lady

A **sweet old lady** in a blue shawl with blue-rinsed grey hair enters. She gives a RED BONBON to **the mandrill** who scarfs it down and proceeds to hiccup happily.

She asks the party questions:

What is your name?

Where are you from?

How heavy are you?

Where are you going?

Will you be visiting the Porcelain Martyrium of St. Jude? Why not?

Are you or have you ever been associated with the Red Church?

Where will you go when you die?

How long will you be staying?

Could St. Jude escape her bondage given suitable Mass?

What gods have you brought with you?

Embellish the questions, add more specific details that she has no reason to ask, but at all times make her the sweetest old lady you have ever met.

If she is asked questions in return the GM should be prepared to improvise. What is her name? Why is she here? Why is she obsessed with mass and the Red Church? Where is she going? How dense is she?

Anyone answering her questions honestly receives A BONBON. She always knows when others are lying and indicates it by not giving them A BONBON. She is kind at all times and politely recommends you save THE BONBONS until after dinner.

Color of Bonbon	Flavor & Effect
Blue	Lavender. Causes instant noticeable weight gain.
Red	Banana. Causes hiccups resulting in multi coloured bubbles for the next hour.
Yellow	Lemon. Counts as a full Provision.
Black	Sesame seeds. Restores 1 point of Luck.
Purple	Liquorice. Dilates pupils and confers +1 Second Sight until the next time you sleep.
Green	Passion fruit. Causes you to hover a few inches above any surface for 2d6 minutes.

If asked about the BONBONS' apparent magic she says she brought them from home. If pressed for more information she giggles and says that an old woman never gives up a recipe just like that!

Keep this going until it gets boring or every character has at least one BONBON at which point they arrive at the next floor as indicated by **the mandrill** giving a single little hoot.

SWEET OLD LADY *SKILL:* **8** *STAMINA:* **8** *INITIATIVE:* **4**

KNITTING NEEDLES (Damage as Knife).

Spells: Befuddle, Brittle Twigs, Grow, Read Entrails.

2nd Floor Passenger: The Gas Form

Outside the door is a CLOUD OF GREEN GAS with little balloon bladders floating in it supporting DECORATIVE JEWELRY much like your ear would. **The mandrill** takes a LITTLE GAS MASK (mandrill-sized only) out from a compartment in the wall by his panel and put it on. If **the sweet old lady** is there she puts her BONBONS away and gets off in a huff as THE GAS FORM enters.

The GAS FORM occupies the entire space. This causes the party to begin to Drown (7.9). Use Strength or Hold Breath to prevent this, Strength representing the energy and willpower to hold your breath where Hold Breath is an Advanced Skill invented on the fly right now by the GM! The journey to the next floor lasts three rounds unless **the mandrill** is convinced to go faster. If the party upsets it it may instead decide to go slower out of spite. If they upset it enough it cites union rules in mandrill-speak and climbs up and out of the lift, leaving the party to their own devices.

Grabbing THE GAS FORM'S JEWELRY can be achieved by Testing your Sleight of Hand. Each party member may attempt to steal instead of resisting Drowning. Each bauble is worth 2D6 PENCE.

THE GAS FORM is a higher life form and doesn't understand solids very well. If the party think to ask it to stop suffocating them, and can improvise smartly or play a convincing game of charades, they may test Etiquette once to see if it understands. If successful it forms a dense ball in the corner until it gets off. This, however, makes its treasures inaccessible.

ADVANCED SKILL: HOLD BREATH

Invent new Advanced Skills when you can't find an existing Advanced Skill situationally appropriate or when the players invent something better. It's as easy as naming something. In this case characters can Test their Hold Breath Skill to hold their breath for longer than normal and resist Drowning or win contests of will.

*GAS FORM SKILL: **10** STAMINA: **20** INITIATIVE: **3***

Spell: Fire Bolt
Immune to physical Damage (Spells inflict Damage as normal).
It is unable to physically hurt anyone other than by suffocating them.

3rd Floor Passenger: Pushy Wall Merchant

The third floor has an alcove set in the wall of the lift shaft. In said alcove is a small shop with all manner of snacks and toiletries pinned to the wall and behind the counter sits a shopkeeper. **The wall merchant** is egg-shaped, with tiny arms barely long enough to reach the top shelves. You cannot see his legs but assume they are equally small. His mouth is alarmingly big, making his AGGRESSIVE SALES PITCHES even more frightening.

WALL MERCHANT SKILL: 5 STAMINA: 6 INITIATIVE: 3

Unarmed since this is a respectable establishment.

Killing the merchant WOULD BE CONSIDERED MURDER at the very least.

THE GAS FORM buys the last packet of *SALT & VINEGAR CRISPS* and floats up the lift shaft on its own, slipping through the bars with ease. THE GAS FORM's pondering over crisp flavours takes an additional Round for Drowning purposes unless that has been resolved.

The wall merchant throws **the mandrill** a small bag of rotten passion fruits which it shovels into its mouth, TEMPORARILY DISTRACTING IT from its duties, including opening the doors.

Other than general snacks and toiletries there are the following items:

- A *PAIR OF RUBY LORGNETTES* for *32P*.
- A *SELECTION OF STUFFED OWLS*. Very lifelike, soft, and poseable. *6P* each.
- A *TRAY OF POCKET GODS* costing *5SP* each.
- A single TIN OF JELLIED PRUNES. Eating them require the imbiber to Test their Luck (or Skill for Enemies) or else feel sick for the day, making them unable to eat or gain the benefits of Provisions. *2SP*.
- A pail of *GOOSE GREASE* costing *15SP*. Very slippery.
- *SMELLING SALTS. 3SP* per vial.

The merchant will keep slipping **the mandrill** old fruit until the party buys something. If the characters get violent brass shutters drop from the ceiling and THE MANDRILL GETS MAD at being cut off from the source of his rancid fruit.

4th Floor Passenger: Too Many Tigers

As soon as the doors open a scrawny woman in a thick leather apron starts pushing tigers into the lift. There are more in the hallway but she says not to worry, she'll wait for the next one.

THREE TIGERS are in the lift, awkwardly squeezed in with the characters. They are crouched or standing against walls, trying to fit in however they can. They are well behaved as long as the characters don't panic or interact with them in an aggressive or fearful way. *The mandrill* starts yanking on a tail, annoying a tiger, but ultimately is ignored.

TIGER *SKILL:* **8** *STAMINA:* **12** *INITIATIVE:* **2**

Damage as Large Beast.

Sometimes it is best to do nothing.

5th Floor Passenger: Mysterious Friend

A new tiger trainer is outside the door pushing tigers around. He takes his tigers off the lift and into a hotel room. If they are dead he insists the party help him carry them into the room since it's most likely their fault. They miss the lift if they do and if they don't he throws his tiger taming chair at them as the door is closing, forcing one random target to Test their Luck (or Skill for Enemies) or take Damage as Club.

Once the doors are closed the characters notice a mysterious presence. Standing betwixt them is a *mysterious friend* who snuck on without anyone noticing, even if everyone watched the door carefully. The *mysterious friend* is small, covered in BRIGHTLY PAINTED ARMOUR from head to toe, and carries a BRIGHTLY COLOURED LANCE. There is no telling what is beneath the ARMOUR.

MYSTERIOUS FRIEND *SKILL:* **9** *STAMINA:* **12** *INITIATIVE:* **2**

Heavy Armour 3.

Lance (Damage as Spear).

The mysterious friend says nothing, but motions enthusiastically. When happy it claps its metal hands together and when hungry it rubs its little metal tummy. *The mysterious friend* follows the party whether they like it or not and can, if they choose to allow it, be used as A HENCHMAN from now on (5.4). It defends and helps them as best it can while always being sure to keep its Armour in a fresh coat of paint.

The GM is recommended to play *the mysterious friend* as sincerely enthusiastic to be the players' companion while also entirely unfamiliar with anything, as though it appeared fully formed that day. The origin and purpose of this little thing is for you to decide.

The Stairs

Ground Floor Stairway

The stairway is the same at each floor: a white-red marble landing separates the way up and the way down as applicable. The stairs themselves are ornate aluminium spiral stairs, each step depicting in relief one of the scenes below. At every encounter the party has the option of leaving the stairway and moving to the lift through the body of the hotel.

Possible ornate stair scenes:

- *The Feeding of St. Eckle:* a huge amorphous figure lurks in one corner and there are figures walking into his open mouth wearing looks of religious ecstasy upon their faces.
- *The Exchange of Mathas:* two beak-faced figures in robes and pointed hats exchange huge serrated keys while shaking hands. Behind each of them hovers a hoard of braying demons.
- *The Reentry of the Starlight:* a smooth orb descends from the sky as people flee the scene.
- *The Many Deaths of Jeremy Bushmoney:* a dense collection of unfortunate deaths, by accident or malice, exhibited upon Jeremy whilst he looks quite resigned and, perhaps, even content.
- *Melissa's Cat:* a lovingly rendered cat staring right at the viewer with benign condescension. Its eyes follow you.
- *Pig Father:* a festive looking pig wearing a stovepipe hat stands atop a dining table, engorging itself, while human diners look on, aghast.

1st Floor Encounter: Owls in the Stairwell

An unfortunate series of events has led to one of the stained glass windows of the hotel being left open, allowing A FLOCK OF 6 SPITEFUL OWLS to find its way in. There is a maid here, with a mop and bucket, taking cover in a corner, waving the mop around like a banner to keep THE SWOOPING OWLS at bay. They attack anyone entering the stairwell and as a result some guests have stopped out of range of THE OWLS' ire to discuss the fate of the trapped maid.

THE OWLS' assault ends once a few of them are dead or injured. When they are gone the maid angrily declares it to be his break, leaving his mop and bucket behind as he stamps out into the main floor.

SPITEFUL OWL *SKILL:* **4** *STAMINA:* **4** *INITIATIVE:* **3**
Damage as Small Beast.

2nd **Floor Encounter: Demon Seawater Leak**

The spa on this floor has sprung a leak and FRIGID WATER has been dripping out of a patch on the wall. The stairs are a series of large puddles. Passage is barred by a chain strung from golden cleats in the wall with a notice saying *"Cleaning Underway. Please Forgive Us For Any Inconvenience Caused"* in a jaunty script. There is a sponge floating in one of the larger pools. There are no staff present.

Anyone stepping into THE WATER and not of demonic origin must Test their Luck (or Skill for Enemies) or suffer the kind of debilitating mental anguish that demons value:

D6	MENTAL ANGUISH
Misery	Lay down in THE WATER and moan piteously.
Terror	Run ahead to the next floor in a panic, splashing the person nearest to you unless they successfully Test their Luck.
Hopelessness	Sit down in THE WATER and refuse to move on account of your life being over.
Ennui	Continue as normal but with less enthusiasm. Lose 1d6 Skill until you sleep it off.
Rage	Paralysed with anger, anyone trying to step past you triggers an attack with whatever you're holding in your hands. You can be slapped out of it.
Hunger	Immediately eat all your Provisions and you must be restrained from eating everyone else's.

All results are in effect until someone snaps you out of it. What qualifies as snap worthy is up to the GM.

3rd Floor Encounter: Slug Monarch

AN ENORMOUS SLUG is wedged in the stairway, his FOUR HERALDS warding off guests and a *mandrill porter* carrying towels. No one may violate HIS MAJESTY'S personal space and dignity and be suffered to live!

They fight anyone trying to pass or touch THE MONARCH but they surrender after the second time one of them gets hurt, slipping through the banisters and away down the walls of the stairwell if possible.

SLUG MONARCH SKILL: 4 STAMINA: 12 INITIATIVE: 2
Damage as Large Beast.

Head of the slug royal family, *His Moist Magnificence, King Juniper Jupiter Lexx-Hafwall IV*. He is currently experiencing some distress and is most embarrassed. Assistance would be rudely accepted and meanly rewarded.

SLUG MONARCH HERALD SKILL: 6 STAMINA: 10 INITIATIVE: 2
Damage as Modest Beast.

Doughy slug creatures the size of a mattress, they announce and facilitate the wishes of the slug nobility. They have a tabard bearing the crest of the reigning slug royal family draped across their backs. It is moist.

4th Floor Encounter: Mysterious Strangers

TWO PEOPLE pass on the stairs and nonchalantly exchange identical satchels. One leaves the stairwell and one continues downward. The satchel of the downwardly headed stranger contains a grip of blank papers clumsily torn from a book. The satchel of the one leaving contains a FOLDABLE BLOWGUN with SEVERAL VIALS, each containing a FLUFFY DART.

The papers contain Zed and three random Spells if viewed with Second Sight. FLUFFY DARTS cause anyone hit to Test their Luck (or Skill for Enemies) or fall asleep for one hour.

2 STRANGERS SKILL: 9 STAMINA: 14 INITIATIVE: 3
Pistolet.
Short Sword.

If a Pistolet is fired off in the hotel it is met with a gang of SECURITY MANDRILLS in a couple of minutes who seek to restrain the offender.

5ᵗʰ Floor Encounter: Trans Dimensional Confusion

The stairs grow and shift as the characters enter this area. They are huge in front and fall away behind. The characters must Climb to clamber up while heading downwards is impossible. The exit to the main floor is ringed with AN ALIEN MAW *(SKILL: 8 STAMINA: 20 INITIATIVE: 0)* that sucks and drips and attacks those who pass through it. Just past the exit, the steps separate and A WIDE CARNIVOROUS SKY opens between them. Characters must jump across or otherwise ingeniously traverse these broad gaps OR FALL FOREVER. If a Test (maybe Athletics — open yourself up to options) is the way you go, have them roll once for the entire climb; you don't need to count the steps and punish them for every single one. Abstraction is a tool that streamlines gameplay.

A woman is sleeping on the last step, using a *LARGE BOOK* as a pillow. Around her the landing opens up into green fields and woodlands and other quaint terrain. Waking the woman snaps everything back to a standard hotel stairwell. The wizard (for this is what she is) fell asleep suddenly, without taking precautions, which ALLOWED HER DREAMS TO LEAK. She thanks the characters and gathers up her belongings, including a *BOOK OF SPELLS* which she has not noticed has SOME VERY IMPORTANT PAGES MISSING.

Anyone who died in the dream is sitting on the stairs, waiting for the rest of the party, unharmed. If the party decides to ignore the wizard and instead enter the dream landscape then that is what they do; forget the hotel and explore THE DREAM WORLD of **Madame Belloza** to your heart's content.

MADAME BELLOZA VAN DER CRUFT SKILL: **10** STAMINA: **12** INITIATIVE: **4**
  Spells: Astral Reach, Breach, Cone of Air, Exchange Shape, Peace,
  Slide Skywards, Teleport, Web.

The 6ᵗʰ Floor: Your Destination!

A rhythmic thumping comes from the roof: the Feast is in full swing! Party-goers hang about, using substances, chatting, and engaging in other festive activities. The characters' room is down the hallway, just past some YOUNG PEOPLE PLAYING A COMPLICATED DICE GAME ON AN ANTIQUE RUG. In the room is a single round bed, not quite big enough for everyone to comfortably fit in, upon which sits a *COMPLIMENTARY BASKET OF COLOURFUL BOILED EGGS*.

If the characters investigate the Feast of the Chiliarch on the roof they see similar parties on other buildings. Attendees are eating traditional novelty fondant arrangements and collecting fireworks to launch at other parties nearby. Mingling results in a roll on the *CALLS TO ADVENTURE BOTH HEARKENED AND PROFFERED AT THE FEAST OF THE CHILIARCH* table (pg. 106).

What will they do tomorrow morning while the dustmen are picking up the burnt rockets and smashed cakes? This is where we leave you and yours to enjoy Troika! to its fullest!

Transportation Alternation

The characters may decide that their choice of transportation isn't working out for them. Make it clear that this is a choice they can make and encourage them to grab hold of their limited fates.

Roll 1d2 followed by 1d6 to determine what they encounter as they move through the passages of the hotel floor:

11	1d3 scared tigers looking for food. *Skill:* **8** *Stamina:* **12** *Luck:* **2.** Damage as Large Beast.
12	An intoxicated chaos champion in a state of anxiety. *Skill:* **10** *Stamina:* **20** *Luck:* **3.** Damage as Polearm.
13	1d6 exhausted porters blindly pushing trolleys of room service food. *Skill:* **4** *Stamina:* **7** *Luck:* **1.** Unarmed.
14	2d6 party goers in a festive mood. *Skill:* **5** *Stamina:* **6** *Luck:* **1.** Damage as Knife.
15	An angular individual using obtuse speech patterns, offering employment, and insisting on exchanging room numbers. *Skill:* **16** *Stamina:* **32** *Luck:* **8** *Armour:* **4.** Damage as Gigantic Beast.
16	6d6 wedding guests brawling with the giant groom *Skill:* **8** *Stamina:* **18** *Luck:* **2.** Damage as Club.
21	2d3 children drawing on the walls in glittery crayon. Close inspection reveals them to be a *learnable spell* (determine randomly).
22	Hotel manager shouting at 2d3 goblins who have torn up the floor.
23	A room left open with a meal set out and no one in sight.
24	The floor appears to be entirely abandoned.
25	2d6 mandrill security guards shooting dice.
26	A colourful naked man locked out of his room in dire need of clothes.

Sometimes you have to improvise. Sometimes you won't have enough information. Most encounters are provided with statistics useful in a fight but they needn't be hostile; this is a hotel after all, so consider other things to present to your players. The chaos warrior might be raging with sadness at the latest rejection of his teratic overlord or the abandoned meal's owner might come back and enjoy watching the characters eat it. Consider complications and wrinkles, and err on the side of creativity and bravado.

D3×10 +D6	Calls to Adventure both Hearkened and Proffered at the Feast of the Chiliarch
11	The mad brothers Marcoul and Hedwig have been spotted wearing matching paper hats of scandalous style and unknown origin. Any citizen of taste would quite literally kill to uncover the source, and would be likely to start a bidding war were such information to appear on the market.
12	Fanfaronade Street has been overrun by a highly organised pack of stray cats. The tenants deny it but they all sport scratch marks and a haunted look. They've all begun to crave milk and laps in which to nest.
13	A new shop, THE DEVIL'S PANTRY, has opened and is selling ground devil bones and horns. The Cultural Weekend Society for Cacodemonic Entities finds this (not to mention the shop's name) to be distasteful and would very much like to consume the proprietor in order to send a message.
14	Nostrificance the Mathmologist left the Feast in a hurry after discovering he was and always has been a hard-light scaffold onto which more powerful egos project their ideas. He plans to kill his creator and transform into pure geometry.
15	The basement of the BLANCMANGE & THISTLE is an exact inverted replica of the surface hotel, hideous anti-guests included. If an anti-guest touches their counterpart they both must Test their Luck (or Skill for Monsters) or explode, dealing d66 Damage to everything nearby and weakening structures.
16	A golden barge, THE CURIOUS PUFFIN, is looking for crew members for their next expedition into the hump-backed sky. They promise extensive travel and spiritual nourishment. Znedzy Tartakov, the expedition's sponsor, seeks to catalogue the biological variances among goblins throughout the Spheres.
21	Cockles' BUTCHERS OF DISTINCTION is looking for delivery people. Discretion required, military background preferred.
22	An owl drops a wad of paper into your lap. The message reads "Bring us fresh volovants if you value your secrets" and there is a crude neighborhood map on the back.
23	Word reaches you that the second coming of one god or another is happening a few streets from here at an all night bath house and spa. But which one? The first people to arrive with offerings will undoubtedly be granted eudemonhood.

D3×10 +D6	Calls to Adventure both Hearkened and Proffered at the Feast of the Chiliarch
24	Uleges the Harrow, a rich and lazy lamassu, would be very grateful to whoever brings him a fresh sausage roll. The bagboy rattles his money bag. Sausage has been banned in the city for months now but can be acquired through black market contacts.
25	A glass blowing coven has accidentally created a sentient crystal Sphere. The surprisingly durable orb has bounced up to the roof and is telepathically shouting that, if rescued from the hammer wielding glass blowers, it will reveal its savior's future.
26	A pair of Eaters from Miss KINSEY'S DINING CLUB have their eyes on the mandrill attendants. They would hate to commit such a faux pas as to openly murder and devour the help but would pay handsomely for a subtler approach to procuring their meal.
31	A doorway opens in the middle of the dance floor and a woman with dozens of pockets dives out of it and disappears into the crowd. A moment later 1d6 guards from the UNIVERSITY OF DOORS follow, demanding to know where she's gone. None of the partygoers except for you seem to have seen where she's hiding.
32	An emissary of Duke DeCorticus offers employment in their lord's search for Rare Earths. Silent assassins in black leotards and golden masks observe the exchange from several vantage points.
33	The lead 'dancer' for the band GREEN STUFF is streaking through the crowd, demanding a hook up for klartesh so the majestic lamassu singer can 'get in the groove'. A child with a large flaming lance menaces the party while an otherworldly smoke creature floats above the child's head.
34	Enforcers of the Phoenix Throne have caused a scene with a forceful arrest. The dissident has surreptitiously dropped a copy of 'IN DEFENSE OF THE RIGHTS OF THE DAMNED: A TREATISE ON THE INHERENT ABUSES OF AN UNREGULATED ECONOMY' by Prof. Hamhead Skeletondog.
35	A short, bearded man wearing the raiments of a Befouler of Ponds, named Captain Treacle, is busily soiling the moonshine punchbowl fountain. The mandrills don't seem to mind. Treacle insists that he is simply honouring the traditions of his people.
36	A sculptor in the employ of Marquess Kaila Grüber is busily carving a Golden Barge out of ice, destined to melt by noon the next day. In the crowd are 1d6 art critics, who DO NOT APPROVE of this manifestation of Art.

LG Lift, Ground Floor:
MANDRILL LIFT ATTENDANT
SKILL: **5** *STAMINA:* **10** *INITIATIVE:* **2**
BITE & CLAW as Modest Beast.

L1 Lift, 1st Floor Passenger:
SWEET OLD LADY
SKILL: **8** *STAMINA:* **8** *INITIATIVE:* **4**
KNITTING NEEDLES (Damage as Knife)
Spells: Befuddle, Brittle Twigs,
Grow, Read Entrails.

L2 Lift, 2nd Floor Passenger:
THE GAS FORM
SKILL: **10** *STAMINA:* **20** *INITIATIVE:* **3**
Spell: Fire Bolt.
Immune to physical Damage
(magic does Damage as normal).
Unable to physically hurt anyone
other than by suffocating them.

L3 Lift, 3rd Floor Passenger:
WALL MERCHANT
SKILL: **5** *STAMINA:* **6** *INITIATIVE:* **3**
Unarmed since this is a
respectable establishment.
Killing the merchant WOULD BE
CONSIDERED MURDER at the very least.

L4 Lift, 4th Floor Passenger:
3 TIGERS
SKILL: **8** *STAMINA:* **12** *INITIATIVE:* **2**
Damage as Large Beast.
Sometimes it is best to do nothing.

L5 Lift, 5th Floor Passenger:
MYSTERIOUS FRIEND
SKILL: **9** *STAMINA:* **12** *INITIATIVE:* **2**
Heavy Armour 3.
Lance (Damage as Spear).

1F 1st Floor Encounter:
6 Spiteful Owls
SKILL: **4** *STAMINA:* **4** *INITIATIVE:* **3**
Damage as Small Beast.

2F 2nd Floor Encounter:
Demon Seawater Leak
Anyone stepping into THE WATER
and not of demonic origin must
Test their Luck or suffer the kind
of debilitating mental anguish
that demons value.

3F 3rd Floor Encounter:
Slug Monarch
SKILL: **4** *STAMINA:* **12** *INITIATIVE:* **2**
Damage as Large Beast.

4 Slug Monarch Heralds
SKILL: **6** *STAMINA:* **10** *INITIATIVE:* **2**
Damage as Modest Beast.

4F 4th Floor Encounter:
2 Strangers
SKILL: **9** *STAMINA:* **14** *INITIATIVE:* **3**
Pistolet.
Short Sword.

5F 5th Floor Encounter:
MADAME BELLOZA VAN DER CRUFT
SKILL: **10** *STAMINA:* **12** *INITIATIVE:* **4**
Spells: Astral Reach, Breach, Cone
of Air, Exchange Shape, Peace,
Slide Skywards, Teleport, Web.

6F The 6th Floor:
YOUR DESTINATION!

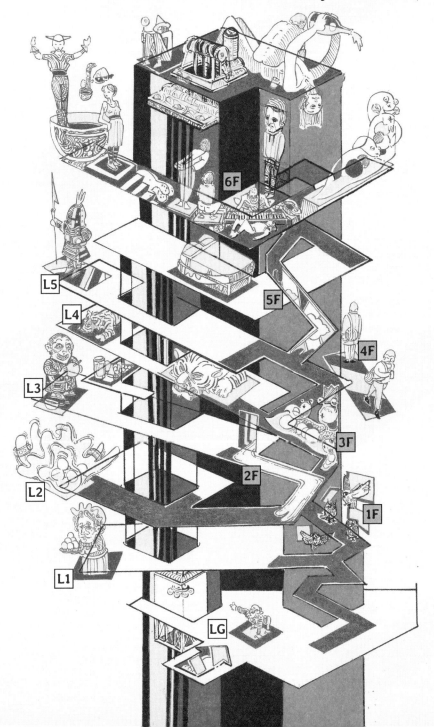

6F

5F

4F

L5

L4

3F

L3

2F

L2

1F

L1

LG

Name

Background

Special

Advanced Skills & Spells

Rank + Skill = Total

Skill

Stamina

Damage

Luck

Spent

Weapons

	Damage						
	1	2	3	4	5	6	7+
_____	☐	☐	☐	☐	☐	☐	☐
_____	☐	☐	☐	☐	☐	☐	☐
_____	☐	☐	☐	☐	☐	☐	☐
_____	☐	☐	☐	☐	☐	☐	☐

Inventory

1 _____

2 _____

3 _____

4 _____

5 _____

6 _____

7 _____

8 _____

9 _____

10 _____

11 _____

12 _____

Wearing

Monies

Provisions

☐ ☐ ☐ ☐ ☐ ☐ ☐
☐ ☐ ☐ ☐ ☐ ☐ ☐

D6×10 +D6	The OOPS! Table
11	There is a flash followed by a shriek — the wizard is now a pig.
12	Twenty-five years of the wizard's life drop away in an instant, possibly making them a very small child. If the wizard is younger than twenty-five they disappear into cosmic pre-birth.
13	A shoal of herring and the water they previously swam in appear above the wizard, soaking everyone.
14	The wizard no longer speaks any known tongue, instead favouring a slightly unpleasant language made up of shrieks and mumbles.
15	The most feared of adolescent academy curses: hiccups! Until dispelled the wizard suffers a -4 penalty to casting.
16	The wizard grows a beautiful tail. If removed it doesn't grow back.
21	All currency in the wizard's possession turns into beautiful butterflies that flap off into the sky.
22	A very surprised orc appears.
23	The wizard catches the Red Eye Curse. Whenever they open their eyes fire shoots out at random as per Fire Bolt.
24	All shoes in the vicinity catch fire.
25	The wizard grows a small pair of horns.
26	All of the wizard's body hair falls out with an audible "fuff!"
31	All Weapons in the vicinity turn into flowers.
32	The wizard's old face melts off and reveals a handsome new one.
33	The wizard disappears in a puff of smoke, never to be seen again.
34	The wizard's hands find a mind of their own and take a severe disliking to the tyranny of control. They set about choking the wizard, only to lapse back into servitude as soon as they pass out.
35	An overflow of plasmic fluid rushes into the wizard's head which expands to the size of a pumpkin. If the wizard is struck for 5+ Damage in one go they must Test their Luck or their head explodes, killing them and dealing 2d6 Damage to anyone standing nearby.
36	A sickness overcomes the wizard, causing them to cough up a thick black fluid. The fluid flows away as though in a hurry to be somewhere. The wizard will soon hear rumours and suffer accusations due to the workings of a sinister doppelgänger.
41	Everyone in the vicinity turns into a pig except the wizard.